MY ANCESTOR WAS A STUDIO PHOTOGRAPHER

by Robert Pols

SOCIETY OF GENEALOGISTS ENTERPRISES LTD.

Published by
Society of Genealogists Enterprises Limited
14 Charterhouse Buildings, Goswell Road
London EC1M 7BA.

© The Society of Genealogists Enterprises 2011.

ISBN: 978-1-907199-06-6

British Library Cataloguing in Publication Data
A CIP Catalogue record for this book is available from the British Library.

All rights reserved
No part of this publication may be reproduced, stored in a retrieval system, or transmitted, in any form, or by any means, electronic, mechanical, photocopying, recording or otherwise, without the prior permission of the publisher and copyright holders.

The Society of Genealogists Enterprises Limited is a wholly owned subsidiary of the Society of Genealogists, a registered charity, no 233701.

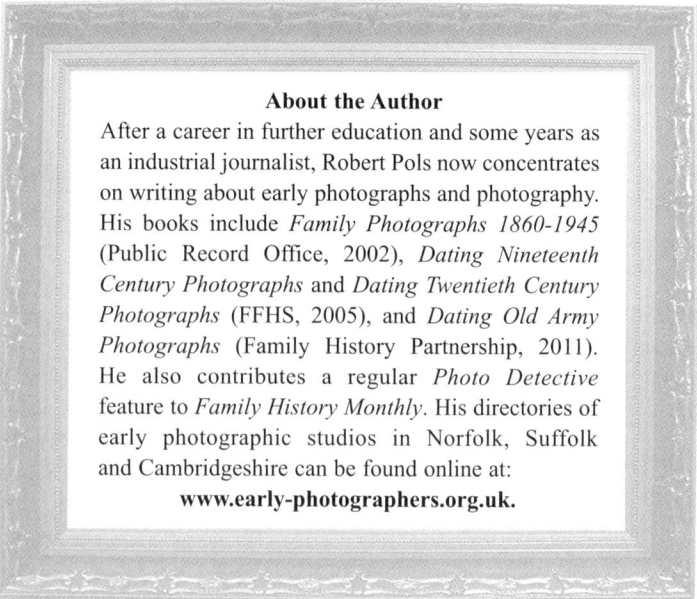

About the Author
After a career in further education and some years as an industrial journalist, Robert Pols now concentrates on writing about early photographs and photography. His books include *Family Photographs 1860-1945* (Public Record Office, 2002), *Dating Nineteenth Century Photographs* and *Dating Twentieth Century Photographs* (FFHS, 2005), and *Dating Old Army Photographs* (Family History Partnership, 2011). He also contributes a regular *Photo Detective* feature to *Family History Monthly*. His directories of early photographic studios in Norfolk, Suffolk and Cambridgeshire can be found online at: **www.early-photographers.org.uk**.

Cover Image - *Self-portrait by Hermann Krone* (1827-1916), 1858. This image is in the public domain because its copyright has expired. Photomontage also features photographs from the Society's Special Collections.

CONTENTS

About the author	ii
Introduction	v
The photographic context	**1**
Conventional sources	**11**
Directories of early photographers	**17**
Printed directories	19
Online directories	26
Photographic chains	29
Online pay-per-view directories	30
Material in archives	**31**
National collections	32
Other repositories: single-studio collections	36
Online repositories	52
Single items in repositories	54
Career and biographical information in print	**57**
Single-studio works	57
Multi-studio works	65
Career and biographical information online	**73**
Single-studio sources	73
Multi-studio sources	78
Periodicals and serial publications	**87**
Photographic societies	**93**
Exhibitions	**101**
Visiting	**105**

The photographs themselves	**109**
Finding examples	110
Photographic mounts	111
The images	123
Additional websites	**143**
General bibliography	**151**
Index of photographers	**156**
General index	**160**

INTRODUCTION

'Let them be well used, for they are the abstract and brief chronicle of the time.' (Shakespeare, *Hamlet*, Act II, scene ii.)

Photography was one of the wonders of the Victorian world, and its practitioners held up a mirror in which the age could see itself. They were a mixed lot: artists, scientists, entrepreneurs, shopkeepers, amateur psychologists, pillars of the community, conmen, visionaries, plodders and much more. Some dabbled briefly in the trade before trying their luck in another field; others built up a business that was to turn into a dynasty. Some enjoyed careers that stretched over decades; others cut short their labours by blowing themselves up or poisoning themselves with the fumes of their chemicals. Most spent their years producing run-of-the-mill portraits of ordinary people, unaware of how valued those portraits would become to later generations. Just a few became famed for the quality of their work or for the distinction of their sitters. Yet even they are better known today by their images than their names. Though many people are familiar with photographs of Brunel on the deck of the *Great Eastern* or Queen Victoria seated on Fyvie and attended by John Brown, few of them know who took the pictures. But however distinguished or unremarkable individual photographers were, as a body they offer us a view into the past. To rescue a photographic ancestor from oblivion is, therefore, an act of social as well as filial piety.

The target reader

In 1851 there were, according to the census, 51 photographers in Britain. By 1861 their numbers had risen to nearly 3,000 and in 1871 the total had risen to over 4,700. Admittedly, not all of these were running businesses in their own right. But if a name over the door is the key criterion, the PhotoLondon database (of which more in due course) has almost 6,000 entries for photographers in the London area between 1841 and 1901. So, if one allows for the passage of three or four generations and assumes a fairly standard rate of reproduction, it follows that early photographers now have many thousands of direct descendants (and many more living relatives at varying degrees of removal). It is at them that this book - as its title suggests - is primarily aimed. But there are also photographic historians, who investigate practitioners and studios without the spur of family connection. Their efforts have created many of the sources to which this book refers. My own understanding of early photographs and photographers has benefited enormously from their work, and those I have encountered have been generous in sharing information. It is my diffident hope that some of them might find something useful in these pages. Last, but most numerous of all the potential readers, are those people whose ancestors had their portraits taken. Family historians are increasingly discovering that it can be helpful to know a little about the studios their forebears visited. Awareness of the market segment a studio served, for instance, can suggest something of a sitter's social status or aspirations. But more particularly, many family historians are recognising the value of studio information in dating their old photos. For them, 'Directories of early photographers' is likely to be the chapter of first resort.

Researching photographers

The study of photographers has its own peculiar features. I can think of no large group of ancestors whose work has survived in such copious and personally identifiable amounts. The field a family labourer ploughed may still be there, but the furrows are new and the grain was turned into bread that has been long since eaten. We can rarely hold the linen our ancestor bleached or the shoe he made, and we certainly can't hold the pig he reared or the ditch he dug. Only occasionally can we point to the ledger he filled or the roof he tiled. An ancestral painter, architect, writer or musician may have produced some identifiable and long-lived work, but not in the profusion achieved by a photographer.

It is immensely satisfying to hold and examine the work of an ancestor (or, at least, work produced in his studio, under his supervision and to his standards). The frustration comes, all too often, with the recognition that the work has survived undocumented. Other sources are tried, in the hope of learning something of the photographer's career. But though the search may turn up further examples of his work in illustrated books or picture libraries, personal papers or business archives are usually harder to come by. In fact, surprisingly little is known about the lives of studio photographers. They kept records, of course: books had to be balanced, stocks had to be ordered, and negatives had to be found when further prints were required. 'Copies may be had at any time' was a standard boast on photographic mounts and in advertisements, and such a boast could not be lived up to without some kind of negative storage and retrieval system. But few such records have survived.

It would be natural to seek out the archives of a trade or professional body, but the possibilities are limited. The records of the Royal Photographic Society can be of interest in many cases, but by no means all photographers joined. There is also a British Institute of Professional Photographers, but that was not formed until 1901. Its archives have been preserved and are in safekeeping, but they are not at present available for public inspection.

It must be accepted, too, that there are photographers who simply don't figure in such records as have survived. Some spent their working lives in the employ of others, so their names never achieved recognition. Some attempted to set themselves up in the business but quickly reverted to their former activities or tried new ones. Some operated as itinerants, working from street to street or country fair to country fair, but never occupying permanent premises or having their own photographic mounts printed. The Scarborough studio of Oliver Sarony provides an extreme illustration of the invisible photographic worker problem. His Gainsborough House premises had 98 rooms and employed in its heyday up to 110 people. But the business was known by only Sarony's name.

The picture so far painted may seem a little bleak. Despite the problems, however, there is material waiting to be discovered, and the aim of this book is to support the process of discovery. I should, therefore, describe the parameters I have set myself.

Defining terms

Some photographers spent only a short part of a working life in the trade. Some spent only a small proportion of a photographic career in a high street shop. Some ran a photographic business for many years, but ran it alongside some other enterprise. All of these have as much claim to be considered as those who spent decades producing nothing but studio portraits. So a studio photographer is, for the purposes of this book, defined as one for whom commercial studio work represented at least one strand or phase of a career. This allows the inclusion of such practitioners as Henry Peach Robinson and Frank Meadow Sutcliffe, who are now often seen primarily as photographic artists rather than everyday retailers of likenesses. It allows, too, for the inclusion of someone like Paul Martin, whose best known pictures date from his amateur days before he opened a studio.

The products of commercial studios varied. Many photographers supplemented portraiture with the making of topographical or architectural images, which they offered for sale to the general public in the form of single prints or stereoscopic cards. Some of these came to specialise - especially in the postcard era of the early twentieth century - as publishers of 'views'. Since, like the pure portraitists, they were supplying a high street product, it has seemed reasonable to relax the definition of studio photographer to include them.

There remain, however, a number of photographers who do not seem to qualify. The genteel amateur and the uncompromising art photographer - who, like Julia Margaret Cameron, were sometimes one and the same - are excluded. Both categories are of importance to the history of photography, but neither depended on it to feed hungry mouths. As photography developed, many specialisms grew up that also fall beyond the boundaries of this book. So there is no attempt to cover (for example) press, fashion, advertising, aerial or scientific photographers - unless, of course, an individual had recognisable high street roots.

In addition to some connection with an essentially retail operation, a qualifying photographer needs to have had a British career dimension. This allows the inclusion both of foreign photographers who worked in Britain and of British-born photographers who spent much or all of their working lives in overseas studios.

Finally, there is a time-scale to be established. The announcement of two different photographic processes in 1839 provides an obvious starting point, though, in practice, the earliest studios date from the 1840s. Settling on a cut-off point is more contentious. I have opted for 1920, and the choice is not entirely arbitrary. Despite the spread of affordable amateur photography in the early years of the twentieth century, studio business remained strong for some time. A decline eventually became noticeable around the time of the First World War, and by the 1920s studios were far fewer in number. Instead, photographic processing was becoming the pressing market need. So the years 1841-1920 cover the heyday of the studio photographer.

But the time-scale has not been slavishly adhered to. A photographer who was active before 1920, and whose career extended into later years, should, I believe, be included. So should a family business that was launched by 1920 and that continued under the family name into later generations. There are also a few pre-1920 businesses that subsequently changed hands and acquired a new name above the door, but that preserved negatives or records of earlier owners. Where such continuity of practice was achieved, rigid insistence on a cut-off point has seemed unreasonable.

In short, criteria have been devised to set some bounds on the scope of this book, but they have been interpreted with a degree of generosity.

Locating Sources

Where libraries, record offices and museums are mentioned in this book, their addresses, telephone numbers and websites are given. But repositories are increasingly becoming parts of networks rather than stand-alone institutions, and some rationalisation of holdings is not uncommon. Items can be stored in one location for production in another, collections can be amalgamated, and buildings can be temporarily or permanently closed. Information about opening times and access to records should, therefore, be checked before a visit is made.

Some of the books and articles referred to are not widely available. For the would-be borrower, the inter-library loans service should be able to solve most problems, though a fee may be payable. Where copies of articles from learned journals are supplied, a copyright fee may also be required. Researchers wishing to possess their own copy of a work may already be aware that certain websites offer a range of titles far beyond the scope of the conventional bookshop. If they have not yet discovered Abe Books (at www.abebooks.co.uk), they might like to know that is a consortium of booksellers with an outstanding offering of obscure and out-of-print titles. There are also some publishers, mainly in the US, that specialise in print-on-demand production of old and rare titles. The best of these books are good-quality facsimiles of the originals; the worst, produced by less-than-perfect optical character recognition (OCR) scanning, can include eccentricities of layout and sudden excursions into gibberish. A few titles from one of the more reliable print-on-demand publishers have been mentioned, and these can be ordered through Abe Books or Amazon (at www.amazon.co.uk).

Many websites are referred to in the text, and the accuracy of their addresses has been rechecked at a late stage in the preparation of this book. But sites sometimes move or undergo reconstruction, acquiring new addresses in the process. Some sites even disappear. If a given web address turns out to have been superseded, and if no redirection is offered, a little creative use of a favourite search engine should usually solve the problem.

Acknowledgements and apologies

There are, of course, people to be thanked and shortcomings to be acknowledged. I am indebted to Mari Alderman, Geoff Caulton, John Frearson, Paul Godfrey, Christopher Pipe and Dr Michael Pritchard for resolving uncertainties or alerting me to new sources. John Frearson has also allowed me to draw on his transcript of the diary written by James Speight while assistant photographer to Jasper Wright. My thanks are due to Else Churchill and Graham Collett, at the Society of Genealogists, for their support and help in turning this project into a book-shaped reality. I am also grateful to my wife, Pam, for her customary willingness to act as sounding board, read drafts and suggest improvements.

As for the shortcomings, the difficulty lies in knowing just what they are. This is, to the best of my knowledge, the first attempt to discuss the study of British studio photographers at such length, and first attempts can always be improved on. I am uncomfortably conscious, therefore, that there must be errors and omissions. I will be happy (as well as sad) to learn of them, and will be anxious to make the necessary changes, should the opportunity of an amended edition arise.

There are, though, two shortcomings that I am aware of, and each could be seen as a case of unfair discrimination. I have, on occasion referred to the photographer as 'he' rather than resorting to repetition of the 'he or she' formula. But it should be stressed that many women worked in studios, both as employees and as principals. They played a significant part in the photographic world and their numbers rose from nearly 700 in the 1871 census to almost 4,000 in 1901. Many worked behind the scenes, but male photographers also valued their presence in the 'operating room' and spoke (not, I think, patronisingly) of their skilful handling of sitters. Of those who ran their own business, some took over from an ailing or deceased husband, but others pursued a long and independent career. My preference for a brief turn of phrase should not be seen as an attempt to diminish their importance. There is probably an imbalance, too, in the selection of photographers chosen to illustrate points being made. If studios in East Anglia - and Norfolk in particular - figure in a disproportionate number of examples, it is because they have been my particular study and I am more familiar with them. The imbalance is not, I hope, repeated in the coverage of sources.

CHAPTER ONE
The photographic context

The aim of this chapter is to provide a background against which individual photographers can be fitted. There is no intention of giving a full history of photography or a detailed account of its processes. The focus is on the development of photography as it affected the studio professional, and the treatment of technicalities will be brief. The result should be an outline that helps the researcher to place a photographer in a context, decide which phases of a changing market he experienced, and judge which processes and formats he dealt with. Further reading, to shed a more searching light on studio practice and working life, can then be found in the bibliography at the end of this book.

The earliest studios

In 1839 photography was given to a wondering world. In fact, it was given twice over. Early in January the daguerreotype process was announced in Paris. Developed by Louis Daguerre, this was a method of forming and fixing images on silver-coated and light-sensitised copper plates. Then in England, on the last day of the same month, William Henry Fox Talbot read a paper to the Royal Society, outlining a system for creating negatives on translucent paper and using them to print positive images. But another two years passed before Britain's first commercial studio was established.

Fox Talbot still had to overcome the problem of half-hour exposures, and it was not until 1841 that he was able to patent an improved process (known as the calotype) and market licences for its use. But his licences were expensive, especially for would-be professionals, and they were taken up by only a few people, most of whom were gentleman amateurs like himself. The ensuing years saw some legal wrangling as Fox Talbot sought to protect his rights and extend them to cover subsequent work by others. As a result, the calotype process did not become a viable commercial proposition. It did, however, incorporate a principle that was in due course to become central to photography.

Daguerre's process, too, was protected in Britain. But Richard Beard acquired the national rights and, in March 1841, opened a studio at the Polytechnic Institute in London's Regent Street. John Goddard was employed to take the portraits and thus became the country's first professional photographer. Beard had also invested heavily in rights that extended far beyond the capital, and he set about selling licences to entrepreneurs who were keen to take the new art into the provinces. These licensees found an eager but select market. Whilst less expensive than a painted portrait, daguerreotypes were not cheap, and only the reasonably moneyed classes could afford them. This limited the number of potential customers in any one town, so most photographers needed to move on with some regularity, making the most of the business opportunity offered by one location before setting out to exploit the next. T H Ely, the Norfolk licensee, commenced operations at the Royal Bazaar in Norwich in December 1843. He moved on to King's Lynn on February 1844, considered venturing across the Cambridgeshire border to Wisbech, and then set up business in Great Yarmouth later in the year. In 1845 he returned to Norwich, taking rooms at a new address, and making a brief excursion to Swaffham. He then disappeared from the record, and by 1846 Beard was seeking a new taker for the Norfolk licence.

Such itinerancy was appropriate for a self-limiting market, and a prolonged career was not necessarily to be expected. But some permanent studios were also established. Antoine Claudet set up London's second studio only months after Beard's Regent Street business opened. Others took longer. Oliver Sarony, for example, travelled extensively before eventually settling in palatial premises in Scarborough.

Obstacles removed

Whilst the daguerreotype represented photography's first commercial success, it was the calotype that foreshadowed its future. The daguerreotype was a one-off image. It was, essentially, a negative that appeared positive only when the light hit it at just the right angle. The calotype was, however, repeatable. The printed copy was made with the aid of a paper negative that could be re-used. But paper, waxed to become translucent, is not the ideal medium for a negative. It is fibrous, and though prints could be made by shining light through it, the results lacked fineness of definition.

In 1851 Frederick Scott Archer introduced his wet collodion process, which involved the creation of negatives on glass. This was to prove the way forward. Transparency was a major improvement on translucency, and the images combined the sharpness of the daguerreotype with the repeatability of the calotype. Moreover, Archer sought to exercise no control over his method, and his generosity lifted the bar to membership of a previously select profession. There were, admittedly, a few years of uncertainty, when wet collodion practitioners were subject to Fox Talbot's attempts to prove the new process infringed his patent, but a test case in 1854 went against him and he chose not to pursue the matter further.

Archer's breakthrough led to a growth in studio practice, despite the difficulties it presented. The glass was coated in collodion, a sticky substance that bound the light-sensitive silver nitrate to the plate. But once the collodion dried, it sealed in the chemical and made it inactive. Coating the glass was, therefore, a last-moment activity, and the photographer then had to work quickly to expose the plate and develop it before the surface hardened. The negative thus formed could be bleached and given a black backing to produce an ambrotype - a one-off positive image on the glass - or it could be placed over a piece of sensitised paper and exposed, developed and fixed to create a repeatable print.

Fox Talbot had used salted paper in the making of his prints, and this was also suitable for prints from the new glass negatives. But it was albumen paper that quickly came to dominate the market. Introduced by Blanquart Everard in 1850, this used the albumen of chickens' eggs as the coating that hosted the photographic chemicals. The albumen dried clear and did nothing to impair the photosensitivity of the surface. From the mid-1860s, the technique of carbon printing was also available. This was based on the principle that some chemicals were hardened (rather than simply darkened) by light, and it offered richness of tone as well as greater permanence of image.

Freedom from licence costs, the opportunity to make and sell more than one copy of an image, and a series of technical improvements made photography attractive to a great number of aspiring exponents. In addition, though portraits made by the wet collodion process were still beyond the financial range of the masses, they could be afforded by a significantly wider section of the public. Many new photographers, therefore, ventured into the arena, and they came (and would continue to come) from a variety of backgrounds. Photography was an activity where art and science met, so, predictably, some of the newcomers had been painters and others had worked in fields requiring technical precision, such as making watches or surgical instruments. But there were recruits all kinds: Ambrose Copsey of Sudbury was a cabinetmaker, Walter Dubisson of Northampton was a draper, and Mrs Charles Bennett of King's Lynn gave lessons in making wax flowers. Many of these new photographers took up the business unreservedly; others kept their two occupations running side by side. (Henry Pendle of Soham followed the triple avocation of photographic artist, sugar boiler and town crier.)

The right format

The greatest expansion of an already expanding market came in the 1860s with the introduction of the carte de visite. These small prints, mounted on card to a final size of 4 x 2½ inches, originated in France, where André Disderi devised a way of creating multiple images on a single photographic plate. Introduced to Britain in the late 1850s, they became popular after John Mayall produced cartes of Queen Victoria and Prince Albert in 1860.

In fact, their success was amazing, and the word 'cartomania' was coined to describe the hold these little pictures took on the public imagination. They were inexpensive, yet the cost covered several copies. Bought by the half-dozen or dozen, pictures could be given to friends and relations while still leaving something to put into the pre-cut apertures of the albums that were quickly designed to hold them. Suddenly great swathes of the population could consider having a portrait, and where a demand exists, people appear on the scene to satisfy the market. The rise of the commercial studio can be followed in trade directories. Kelly's Norfolk directory for 1853 listed no photographers, but four studios were featured in Craven's directory for 1856. In 1858 Kelly recorded 14, and just over twice this number were found by Harrod in 1863, White in 1864 and Kelly in 1865. Harrod's 1868 list of 40 studios represented an increase of 1,000 per cent in a twelve-year period. Over half of the 1868 studios were in Norwich, but there were also six in Yarmouth, four in King's Lynn and two in Thetford, while a further half-dozen were scattered around the smaller centres. Not only could most people now entertain the idea of having a picture taken at least once in their lives; they could also - even in a predominantly rural county - quite easily find a photographer to undertake the task.

The carte de visite held sway for decades, but it was not the only option. In 1866 the rather bigger cabinet print was introduced, though it was not until the later years of the century that it outsold the carte. There were also larger sizes for those able to pay more. A handbill for Sawyer & Bird of Norwich, dating from the 1870s, also advertised full-size, extra-size, crown, royal and imperial. (The imperial prints measured 31 x 26 inches, mounted, and cost 42/-.) Many photographers produced local views for sale, too, sometimes in stereoscopic form. Some created opaltypes (carbon prints on pearly white glass) or Woodburytypes (semi-photomechanical prints suitable for reproduction). Those working in smaller centres of population or targeting the less affluent customers might have a fairly restricted offering, but many photographers were proving very versatile.

At the lower end of the market, there was yet one more kind of photograph that could be made. This was the tintype, known more properly but less commonly - in Britain, at least - as the ferrotype. Introduced in the 1850s, the tintype enjoyed a healthy studio existence in the USA. In Britain, however, it gained few supporters until the 1870s and later, when it became popular amongst itinerants. A one-off image, produced on a thin sheet of chemically-treated iron and developed in-camera, the tintype was cheap to make and needed no special premises for processing. It appealed, therefore, to a new generation of travelling photographers. Whereas previous itinerants had moved about to find customers who could afford an expensive product, their successors took to the road in search of customers who could afford only a cheap one. In addition, they catered for customers at fairs, the seaside and country shows, for whom a photo was a quick and inexpensive reminder of the occasion.

Technical advances

Until the late 1870s most photographers were still coping with the messy and time-sensitive demands of the wet collodion process. Daguerreotypes had been squeezed out of the market by the arrival of the ambrotype, and ambrotypes had lost impetus as the taste for cartes de visite grew (though some surprisingly late examples from the 1880s and even 1890s are occasionally found.) The carte was still the dominant format, though it would eventually be edged onto second place by the cabinet print in the 1880s. Both formats would survive into the early years of the twentieth century. Albumen paper still held sway, with carbon printing set to become more widespread in the century's later years.

But a significant step forward was to be made with the arrival of dry plate printing. The advance was, in fact, remarkably slow, but it was eventually overwhelming. A dry plate process was first attempted in the mid-1850s, and the plates were on sale in England as early as 1860. Their impact was minimal. Then, in 1871, Richard Leach Maddox published an account of his method of preparing photographic plates using a coating of cadmium bromide, silver nitrate and gelatin, which remained light-sensitive when dry. The plates could be factory made, they were easy to store, and they could be used in the field without the need for a portable darkroom. Take-up was slow, partly because the relatively expensive plates could not, like collodion plates, be scraped clean and reused. But in 1878 Charles Bennett produced plates with much greater sensitivity to light. This was the decisive factor. Exposure times were dramatically reduced, processing was now much more convenient, and the wet collodion process quickly became obsolete.

Since photography had become so much less dependent on the practitioner's chemical skills, a further dramatic increase in the numbers wishing to try their hand might have been expected. But expansion of the profession was not great. In some areas the number of studios levelled out, and in some it dropped slightly. Overall, growth continued, but it was fairly steady. Photography had reached nearly every level of society, and there was no obvious direction in which to expand. Business growth could reflect population growth, or clients could be persuaded to visit the photographer more frequently. But the studio boom of the 1850s and 1860s couldn't continue at such a high level.

Some photographers withdrew from the business, but others acquired additional studios and built up modest local chains. There were chains, too, at regional and national levels, and it was in the 1880s that the two biggest multiples, A & G Taylor and Brown, Barnes & Bell, flourished most strongly. Photography could still be very profitable, but it was a competitive business, and the individual had to work hard to win and keep his market share. The gelatin dry plate supported his efforts. The photographer could now more easily take his camera out of the studio, since the plates were prepared in advance rather than wetly managed immediately before exposure to the light. So in the 1880s and early 1890s more and more professionals began to advertise an extended service. William Bond of Norwich advertised 'schools, wedding parties and every class of outdoor work attended to'; Jane MacLean of North Walsham specialised in 'large groups and all branches of outdoor photography'; and Alfred Knighton of Kettering promised prompt attention to 'orders to go out to photograph groups, views, animals, machinery, etc'.

Back inside the studio, new possibilities were opening up in the methods of studio lighting. Photographers had hitherto been dependent on daylight coming through the windows of a generously glazed operating room situated, often, on an upper floor. Working hours had, of necessity, been affected by weather conditions, by the time of year, and by the time of day. Artificial lighting could change all that, and the first electrically-lit studio was announced in 1877. But the spread of mains electricity was slow and uneven, and, unless they installed their own generators, many practitioners had to wait before making the change. In the mid-1880s

Matthew Boak of Bridlington was able to draw customers' attention to the convenience of a ground-floor studio, and by 1890 William Shrubsole was in a position to offer twelve-hour opening at both his Norwich premises. Jasper James Wright had to wait until the autumn of 1899 for electricity to reach King's Lynn, but he was keen to adopt the new lighting as soon as possible and this probably provided the motivation for the new studio he had fitted early in the next year. But not all photographers were so anxious to adapt. Some preferred the softness of natural light, and William Hayes of Hutton-le-Hole resisted the change until after the First World War.

There were also technical advances that had only limited effect on work within the studio. They did, however, pave the way for the rise in amateur photography at the beginning of the twentieth century. New kinds of printing paper were devised that were easy to use and produce. Ilford Ltd introduced gelatino-chloride paper in England in 1885; the machine production of continuous rolls of collodion printing-out paper was pioneered in Germany in 1889; the American Aristotype Company began to make collodio-chloride printing-out paper in 1889, and the manufacture of gelatin-chloride papers followed in the 1890s. A new generation of photographic papers was being born that would in due course be of use both to amateurs, who wished to print their own pictures, and to professional finishers, who processed the films that amateurs passed to them.

An alternative to the heavy and brittle glass negatives also appeared. Celluloid had been invented by Alexander Parkes as early as 1861, but not until 1888 did John Carbutt of Philadelphia begin to produce the thin, flexible sheets that would be suitable for photographic use. George Eastman, who had already been experimenting with a gelatin-coated, paper-backed roll film, was quick to see the possibilities of celluloid and switch to it. By sealing his new films inside a simple box camera, he could (and did) invite the user to wind the film through a series of exposures before returning the camera, unopened, for processing. To studio photographers, who needed no such outside help, this was of little interest; but it opened up the possibility of photography as a hobby to people who had previously been deterred by its costs, complications and time demands.

The challenge of the amateur

Eastman's great breakthrough came in 1900 with the launch of the Box Brownie. It was startling in its simplicity and in its cheapness. It came, ready-loaded with a film, as a small box fitted with a rotary shutter. The user simply had to point and click. Once the film was finished, the whole package was handed over to professionals for developing and printing. It cost a mere five shillings. Suddenly millions of people could afford to take pictures and had no need to immerse themselves in the arcana that had previously attended the activity. The Box Brownie democratised making photographs in much the same way as the carte de visite had democratised sitting for them.

The rise of the amateur, taking off hesitantly in the late 1880s and soaring in the early 1900s, could have led to an immediate dwindling of studio business. But it didn't. The professionals' product was still distinctly superior: they could take pictures indoors; they could bring the camera closer to the subject; they avoided the problems of sunshine squint and hat-brim shadow; and they contrived to fit people into the frame without cutting off the outside member of a group or the top of the tallest person's head. The studio was still the home of the decent portrait.

Professionals also looked for new ways to compete. Reduced prices and special offers, then as now, were seen as a way to reach the public's heart. In 1885 Thomas Smith of King's Lynn was charging 6/- a dozen for cartes and 15/- for cabinet prints. By 1894 his prices had dropped to 5/- and 12/- respectively, and he was offering a free opaltype with the more expensive cabinet card range.

The willingness to work outside the studio increased. Group photographs became more common, showing members of the same team, class, social organisation or military unit. In the Edwardian period, outdoor pictures of the wedding party became more usual than studio portraits of just the bride and groom. As the holiday market grew, photographers sought to exploit it, sometimes setting up seasonal satellite studios near the beach. So Jasper Wright of King's Lynn opened a studio near the pier at nearby Hunstanton 'during the season', while May Bone, already established some miles inland at Fakenham, set up a beachside kiosk at the same resort. Later, in the 1920s and 1930s, the promenade photographer would flourish, taking pictures of passers-by in the hope of securing a sale. (These photographs were known as 'walkies' in the trade.)

Novelty formats offered another way of competing, and the years around the turn of the century saw the proliferation of novelty-sized prints aimed at rejuvenating a market that had become rather tired of cartes and cabinet prints. The real format success story, though, was the postcard. Early postcards reserved one whole side for the recipient's name and address, but a relaxation of regulations in 1902 allowed message and address to share one side, leaving the other side free for a picture. The idea proved immensely popular, and in the financial year 1903-1904 the postman delivered 700 million postcards in Britain. People enjoyed sending messages enhanced by attractive images, and this proved a perfect opportunity for professional photographers. Those who were already marketing topographical and architectural pictures were able to step up their output, while others were prompted to embark for the first time on publishing scenic views and souvenirs of local events. But the postcard was also suited to the traditional portrait trade. It was the format of the moment, and it provided the inexpensive alternative to cartes and cabinet prints that the market had been waiting for. A photographer still needed, for the first few years of the new century, to retain the old Victorian formats as part of his repertoire: while customers still had empty spaces in their existing albums, there was a demand that it would have been rash to ignore. But the postcard very quickly became the dominant popular format for affordable photographs.

The new century also brought other developments. There was taste for larger mounted prints, when something more formal than a postcard was required. The Lumière Brothers announced (in 1904) and marketed (in 1907) the Autochrome colour process. The First World War created a new call for the services of the professional, since there was a demand for portraits of soldiers leaving home and - in the more fortunate cases - soldiers reunited with their families. But the challenge of the amateur could not be held at bay indefinitely. The role of family photographer was being taken over by the family itself, and the growing requirement was for professional processing rather than professionally taken pictures.

As ever, trade directories can be used to chart the trend. Though studio growth had been slower in the later decades of the nineteenth century, it had continued, and the postcard boom of the early 1900s sustained the trend. Between 1900 and 1912 the total of Norfolk, Suffolk and Cambridgeshire photographers listed by Kelly rose from 139 to 167. But by 1916 a decline had begun, and the total had slipped to 146. The 1925 figure was 123, and only 82 names were listed in 1937.

The photographic studio was, of course, by no means dead; but the great age of the studio photographer was over.

CHAPTER TWO
Conventional sources

Genealogists are already familiar with the usual ways of finding out about an ancestor. All that is needed on most of the conventional sources, therefore, is a few passing thoughts.

Talking to relations

It is customary to interview elderly relatives to glean snippets from the past, and such interviews are commonly accompanied by a request for a sight of old family photos. When a photographer is the object of interest, this request needs to be broadened to include photographs of any kind from the ancestor's studio. It is important, in such cases, to see and copy whole photographs, front and back, for the mounts can prove useful sources of information. Unfortunately the current trend is to exchange scans of pictures, and information can be lost as a result. Photographs may be cropped to concentrate on the image and cut out the surround; or they may be printed out to a size that is offered by the computer software, but that makes it difficult to determine the format of the original. Researchers should therefore seek to know a picture's original size and how it was presented, and they should beg for a copy of the reverse of any cardboard mount as well as a copy of the image on its face. (What can be learned from mounts is discussed in a later chapter entitled 'The photographs themselves'.)

Vital records and censuses

The occupation of 'photographer', as stated on a census return or a certificate of birth, marriage or death, is no guarantee of a corresponding studio. Some photographers spent part or all of their careers in somebody else's business. Others worked as itinerants, without having fixed long-term premises. A few ran their operation under a name other than their own. (Bert Armond Taylor of Great Yarmouth, for example, called his business the Orient Art Company.)

Researchers should also be aware that a photographer's occupation could be recorded in a number of different ways. The principal of a business might, in the early years especially, be recorded as 'photographic artist', 'photographic portrait taker', 'daguerreotypist' or 'daguerreotype artist'. An employee might appear as 'retoucher', 'finisher' or 'colourist', according to the stage of processing in which he or she specialised.

Assumptions about addresses should be guarded against. The home address may or may not have been the location of a studio.

Newspapers

Unless a photographer achieved particular eminence, he is more likely to have been noticed by the local than the national press.

Many local newspapers survive, both in their own areas and in the British Library's collection at Colindale, and identifying potentially helpful publications is not difficult. In 1988 a project called Newsplan was established to catalogue, preserve and microfilm local newspapers throughout the UK. It is divided into ten regions, most of which now have comprehensive online catalogues. (The West Midlands is, at the time of writing, the one exception.) As an aid to locating holdings, Newsplan is invaluable. Each region has its own online search facility, but the home page of the North of England Newspaper Archive (at www.n-e-n-a.co.uk/newsarchives.php) is particularly useful: it provides a good overview, offers brief descriptions of what each region has to offer, and provides links to all the other Newsplan websites.

Though identifying publications is relatively simple, deciding on target issues is much more difficult. In the highly probable absence of an index, the researcher will have to decide on likely dates and be prepared to wind through wearisome reels of microfilm. Death notices and obituaries will usually be the most promising sources, since it is possible to start the search at a known date. (Obituaries, remember, may appear less promptly than death notices.) Otherwise, discovery of a relevant item may depend largely on tenacity or luck. It may, though, be worth considering occasions when a photographer might have been most likely to place an announcement or an advertisement. The launch of a new business, the move to a new address, the adoption of a new process or the introduction of a new format might all be reasons for seeking to catch the public's attention. The conversion of a studio to electric lighting may also have been thought worthy of comment. Though the earliest electrically lit studio appeared in 1877, many towns (and many photographers) had to wait until the 1890s for the arrival of a mains supply.

Photographers often became prominent members of their local community, so there is always the chance of finding the desired name mentioned in reports covering civic events, or the activities of churches, business associations and fraternal societies. Nor should one ignore those literary, philosophical and scientific societies to which the Victorians were so attached. Local newspapers have the potential, therefore, to be the researcher's oyster, but they can be a major test of stamina. Pearls, after all, take a long time to produce, and the process entails a lot of gritty irritation.

Directories

Blemished by inaccuracies and out of date before they appeared, trade directories can nevertheless contribute significantly to the stock of information. Over the years they can provide an outline of a photographer's career, flagging up studio moves and business partnerships. Because they tend to give the same information as photographic mounts, they can also be helpful in dating old photographs. Both of these functions depend on being able to consult a series of directories, and this has led to trade directories being used to create directories of studio photographers. This subject will be explored in the next chapter. But individual trade directories also have their value, and they sometimes include material that compilers of photographer directories have not extracted.

In the earlier directories, photographers must be sought in the general lists of tradesmen that are appended to the articles on individual towns. Later, these town lists start to be sorted under occupational headings, and eventually (in countywide directories) lists for the whole area are given alphabetically, occupation by occupation. But not until well into the 1860s is it safe to assume that it's enough to look for the category of 'Photographer'. As with censuses and vital records, a number of terms can be used, though the most likely variant heading proves to be 'Artist'. (It is common to find, under the 'Artists' heading, names that are followed by 'photographic' in brackets.)

Directories generally contained some pages of advertisements, and a photographer or two is often to be found among them. When an advertisement is discovered, it can turn out to be full of information. So Alfred Knighton of Kettering, in an 1890 directory, assured the public of his willingness to work outside the studio. He was keen to retain the associations of 'photographic artist', while reassuring clients that he used the latest modern process. He stressed versatility ('in all the different styles'), value for money ('moderate charges') and businesslike efficiency ('all orders ... promptly attended to'). He offered enlargements and colouring, and he had ventured into publishing with 'local views for sale'. Finally, he appended a list of distinguished patrons, beginning with the Princess of Wales and including a duke, two earls and a selection of lords, ladies, honourables and reverends. It all amounts to an insight into Knighton's mind as he sought to position himself in the market.

Most photographers had no more than their simple list entry, but even that could be revealing. What often emerges is evidence of photographers reluctant to abandon the trade they had formerly practised and keen to maintain a diversity of activity. So William Fisher of Great Yarmouth still presented himself as an optician in 1859, five years or more after setting up a studio; Peter Davies of Ely was also listed in 1873 as a pharmaceutical chemist and an oil and colour man; and Thomas Howard of Wells-next-the-Sea was revealed in 1863 as a printer and the owner of a gasworks.

The other use of directories is for examining whole streets and understanding the location in which a photographer carried on his trade. A similar exercise can be undertaken with census returns, but, for this purpose, a directory's focus on traders may be more helpful than a census' concern with inhabitants. By looking at the surrounding businesses one can develop a sense of the neighbourhood, judging perhaps whether its occupants were catering to the upper or lower end of the market. Some streets had a more stable trading population than others, and that can be discerned from a series of directories. Other streets held a particular attraction for photographers and were home to a series of studios over the years. (Glasshouse Street in London was home to so many studios that it was named after them.) If a street seems to have been particularly favoured by photographers, it may be because it was seen as a 'good' address, or there may have been a geographical reason. Many photographers set a high value on north-facing windows, which provided even illumination without dazzling glare. Streets that lay on an east-west line offered the possibility of north-light studios at either the front or the back, and corner sites of north-south streets might also offer opportunities for north-light illumination. (A street map, used in conjunction with a street directory, could reveal whether an ancestor had this popular lighting option open to him.)

Examination of a sequence of directories can bring its own insights. Moves from one studio to another may suggest the possibility of upward or downward social mobility. It may become clear whether a photographer began business in an established studio location or had to bear the cost of setting up a completely new operation. It might be interesting to note whether the previous occupier disappeared from photographer lists, drew in his horns and moved to a less select area, or had prospered so well that he moved on to a more desirable address. The question then is how the ancestral photographer seems to have fared in comparison with his predecessor.

Finding a selection of directories should pose no great problems. If a visit to the appropriate area is possible, the holdings of local libraries and archives should be worth investigating. In London there is a very good national collection at the Society of Genealogists and a more locally focused collection at the Guildhall Library. For those wishing to search online, there is an impressive (and indexed) collection of directories on the website of the University of Leicester's Historical Directories project (www.historicaldirectories.org/hd). Material from directories is also currently being amassed online at www.familyrelatives.com/index.php. Their directories can be searched (for a fee) rather than browsed, and, at the time of writing, some counties are not represented and few are covered by more than one volume. But the site may have its uses, as its database grows.

Researchers should not, however confine themselves to full-scale county and town directories. All kinds of local almanacs, annuals and civic or trade promotional publications were produced. Some were linked to newspapers. They were much less ambitious in scope, but they can prove useful sources of information and, especially, advertisements. Their titles varied, and there's no way of predicting what any one town's publication might be called. King's Lynn had a *Red Book*, Ely had a *Creak's Almanack* and Great Yarmouth had a *Fingerpost*. Fortunately books and booklets of this kind tend to be placed alongside fully-fledged directories in library collections, so that discovering them is not simply left to chance.

Sources at the Society of Genealogists

The society's library has no special focus on photographers, but - as for anyone else of any occupation - it may hold material that is of interest. It does, as already mentioned, have a good collection of trade directories, and it holds a modest selection of works related to photography. Where one of these is mentioned in this book, its library shelf mark - flagged by the abbreviation 'SoG' - is added in square brackets.

Researchers may also decide to search the county shelves for books containing old photographs of specific localities. These have earned their library place on the strength of their local interest, but, since professionals often took a camera outside their own premises, they will often contain examples of the work of studio photographers. If such a book has an index, it should, of course, be checked. If there is no index, there should be captions, photographer credits or acknowledgements of photographic sources. An example of his work may not say much about a photographer (though a later chapter will argue that it sometimes can), but any evidence of a photographic ancestor is likely to be welcome. Some books of this kind organise their photographs around themes, and trade is a popular subject. So it occasionally happens that a picture of a studio's shop front is found.

In theory, local histories could also repay investigation. They may contain attributed photographic illustrations, and, since photographers often came to be prominent members of their community, they may even include mention of the studio. In practice, however, such books should probably be read for their general local interest, with any reference to a photographic ancestor being seen as an unexpected bonus.

Archives and record offices

There is much relevant material to be found at the National Archives, the British Library, county record offices, museums and local studies libraries. They are the one conventional source about which there is much to be said, and their holdings are considered in a later chapter. Except for a brief discussion of a handful of national collections, however, that chapter is organised around categories of evidence rather than around the places where the evidence is stored.

CHAPTER THREE
Directories of early photographers

In theory, trade directories are useful for tracing the career of anyone running a small business, but there is a distinctive bonus in the case of photographers. They habitually printed their business name and address on the back of their products, and millions of those products have survived. The trade details on a particular photographic mount can therefore be compared with a series of known (and roughly datable) studio names and addresses. So lists of an area's early photographers - drawn from trade directory entries and recording business names and studio addresses - can be of particular use both to researchers of individual professionals and to those seeking to date the photograph of an ancestor. The former can establish a broad career outline, noting studio moves, business expansion, and partnerships with family members or other professionals. The latter can check which period of years coincides with the information given on their heirloom's mount.

A to Z lists (or directories) of early photographers exist for many parts of Britain, but coverage is still patchy. It also takes various forms. There are county directories, part-county directories and town or city directories. Counties are generally defined in terms appropriate to the period covered, but this is not invariably the case. (Two Welsh directories, for instance, are based on the county groupings that resulted from the Local Government Act of 1972.)

The value of listings derived from trade directories is readily seen. Some photographers stayed resolutely in the same studio year after year, but many did not: they moved to new locations; they took on additional premises and sometimes later gave them up; they formed and dissolved partnerships; they took other family members into the business. Such changes tend to be reflected in trade directories, which offered commercial information in the form in which a photographer would advertise himself, rather than personal information in the way a census would record. In addition, trade directories appeared much more frequently than censuses. A publisher often followed a more-or-less four-yearly cycle, and there was always a good chance that a competitor would time his volumes to fill the gap. A series of directories, therefore, represents a time-lapse record of an area's businesses with which ten-yearly censuses cannot compete.

But there is, of course, a downside. Trade directories have their shortcomings. They were not paragons of accuracy, and some publishers were less meticulous than others. Information was generally assembled well in advance, and some directories had a longer time lag between the collection and publication of material than others. So a studio could be established a year or more before its name first appeared in print, and it could cease trading some while before or after its last directory mention.

In spite of these reservations, photographer directories based on trade directory information can be enormously useful. They simply have to be used thoughtfully, maintaining an awareness of their limitations and avoiding conclusions that are too precisely dated. The best photographer directories come with just such a warning, and researchers will find it relatively easy to judge their merits: the more extensive its sources and the shorter the gaps between them, the more helpful a listing is likely to be.

Some listings, too, offer added value in one way or another. There may be comments on apparently unreliable evidence; there may be additional information from trade directories, photographic mounts, census returns or other sources. Publications by the Royal Photographic Society generally indicate where premises changed hands from one practitioner to another. Some compilations offer a number of photographer profiles to supplement the lists of dates and addresses.

The launch of a number of online photographer directories has helped improve geographical coverage significantly. There will, however, be researchers whose locality of interest has not yet been tackled. They could consider compiling their own list, checking a series of trade directories for their target photographer. (Locating collections of trade directories is discussed in the earlier chapter on 'Conventional sources'.) Working through a sequence of sources for a single photographer should not be too time-consuming. Any researcher deciding to compile, at the same time, a full studio list for the town or county in question would be doing a valuable service.

1. Printed directories

Most of the printed directories were compiled by members of the Royal Photographic Society (RPS) - who were the pioneers in this field - and issued as supplements to *The PhotoHistorian*, the magazine of the society's Historical Group. These have been appearing since the late 1970s and all (it is hoped) are mentioned below. It will be apparent that some are revisions of earlier versions. A list of those currently available can be found on the Historical Group's website at www.rps.org/group/Historical/PhotoHistorian--Supplements, and researchers wishing to order copies are invited to email the Group Secretary. (The secretary at the time of writing is Jenny Ford, and the address is jennyford2000@yahoo.co.uk. But, as with any organisation, officers can change, so it would be wise to double-check this information by visiting the above-mentioned web page.)

RPS directories present problems for bibliographers. Some give Bath as the place of publication; a few give London; many remain silent. The British Library opts for London for the whole series. In this book, therefore, London has been given as the location, except in those cases where I have been able to ascertain that Bath is named on the publication itself. Titles, too, seem to have been modified over the years, with a number of abbreviated versions appearing in the current RPS catalogue.

Some directories could prove difficult to locate. The Paisley directory, printed as a limited edition, is particularly elusive, though it is listed for the sake of completeness. But many titles, including some RPS lists that are not currently available, can be found in the excellent collection of photographer directories at the Guildhall Library in London. (Contact details are: Guildhall Library, Aldermanbury, London, EC2V 7HH; 020 7332 1868; www.cityoflondon.gov.uk/ Corporation/LGNL_Services/Leisure_and_culture/Libraries/City_of_London_libr aries/guildhall_lib.htm.)

England

Berkshire
Cannon, P, *A directory of photographers: Newbury and district 1854-1945* (Newbury: Newbury District Museum, 1997) [SoG shelf mark: Berkshire Tracts Box].
Smith, Mervyn L, *Photographers in Abingdon 1863-1909* (London: RPS, *PhotoHistorian* Supplement 44, 1979).

Buckinghamshire
Doig, Tom, *A new look at photography: Bucks photographers* in *Bucks Ancestor*, volume 15, number 1 (Haddenham: Buckinghamshire Genealogical Society, March 2006) [SoG shelf mark: BU/PER].

Cambridgeshire
Rouse, Michael, *Cambridgeshire in early postcards* (Cambridge: Oleander Press, 1978).

Cheshire
Jones, Gillian A & Graham, *Professional photographers in Cheshire 1849-1940* (London: RPS, *PhotoHistorian* Supplement 108, 1995).

Cornwall
Thomas, Charles, *Views and likenesses: early photographers and their work in Cornwall and the isles of Scilly* (Truro: Royal Institution of Cornwall, 1988).

Derbyshire
Adamson, Keith I P, *Professional photographers in Derbyshire 1843-1914* (London: RPS, *PhotoHistorian* Supplement 118, 1997).

Devon
Scott, C G, *Photographers in Devon 1842-1939* (London: RPS, *PhotoHistorian* Supplement 101, 1993).

Dorset
Hallett, Michael, *Victorian and Edwardian professional photographers in Dorset 1855-1920* (London: RPS, *PhotoHistorian* Supplement 76, 1987).

Durham
(See Northumberland.)

Essex
Appleby, David & John, *Professional photographers in Colchester and North Essex 1845-1931* (London, RPS, *PhotoHistorian* Supplement 95, 1991).
Appleby, David & John, *The magic boxes: professional photographers and their studios in North Essex 1845-1937* (Chelmsford: Essex Record Office, 1992) [SoG shelf mark: ES/PER].

Gloucestershire
Hallett, Michael, *Professional photographers in Cheltenham 1841-1914* (Bath: RPS, *PhotoHistorian* Supplement 75, 1986).

Hallett, Michael, *Victorian and Edwardian professional photographers in Gloucester 1857-1914* (London: RPS, *PhotoHistorian* Supplement, 1988/1989).

Vaughan, Roger, *Nineteenth and twentieth century professional photographers in Bristol* (London: RPS, *PhotoHistorian* Supplement 156, 2008).

Hampshire

Norgate, Martin, *Directory of Hampshire Photographers* (Winchester: Hampshire County Council Museums Service, 1995).

Herefordshire

Hallett, Michael, *Professional photographers in Herefordshire 1852-1910* (London: RPS, *PhotoHistorian* Supplement 91, 1990).

Hertfordshire

Pritchard, Michael, *Victorian and Edwardian photographers in Watford 1862-1913* (London: RPS, *PhotoHistorian* Supplement 45, 1980).

Smith, Bill & Pritchard, Michael, *Hertfordshire photographers 1839-1939* (Stevenage: Smith & Pritchard, 1985).

Lancashire

Forrest, David, *Warrington photographers 1854-1992* (Liverpool: Liverpool & SW Lancashire FHS, 1993).

Gee, Ian & Rendell, Douglas, *Professional photographers in Altrincham and Sale* (London: RPS, *PhotoHistorian* Supplement 88, 1990).

Hannavy, John & Ryan, Chris, *Professional photographers in Wigan 1853-1925* (London: RPS, *PhotoHistorian* Supplement 78, 1987).

Jones, Gillian, *Lancashire professional photographers 1840-1940* (Watford: PhotoResearch, 2004).

Linkman, Audrey, *Manchester Photographers 1901-1936* (Manchester: Documentary Photography Archive, 1988).

Linkman, Audrey, *Professional photographers in Liverpool 1850-1900* (London: RPS, *PhotoHistorian* Supplement 98, 1992).

Liverpool & SW Lancs FHS, *Warrington photographers 1854-1992* (Liverpool: Liverpool & SW Lancs FHS, 1992).

Read, Gillian, *Manchester photographers 1840-1900* (London: RPS, *PhotoHistorian* Supplement 59, 1982).

Smith, Mervyn L, *Professional photographer supplement: Altrincham 1860-1939* (London: RPS, *PhotoHistorian* Supplement 44, 1979).

Leicestershire

Heathcote, Pauline & Bernard, *Leicester photographic studios in Victorian and Edwardian times 1844-1910* (London: RPS, *PhotoHistorian* Supplement, 1982).

Wilshere, Jonathan, *Leicester portrait photographers before 1900* (Leicester: Research Section of Chamberlain Music and Books, 1988).

Lincolnshire
Adamson, Keith I P, *Professional photographers in Lincolnshire 1844-1900* (London: RPS, *PhotoHistorian* Supplement 99, 1993).
Swithinbank, J S, *Early professional photographers in Grimsby* in *Lincolnshire Life* (Grimsby: Lincolnshire Life Limited, April 1982).

London/Middlesex
Pritchard, Michael, *A directory of London photographers 1841-1908* (Watford: PhotoResearch, 1986, revised and expanded 1994) [SoG shelf mark: MX/G 275 and PR/PHO].
Webb, David, *The photographers of Regent Street, London 1841-1901* (London: RPS, *PhotoHistorian* Supplement 128, 1999).
West, John, *The studio photographers of the London Boroughs of Lewisham and Greenwich 1854-1939* (London: RPS, *PhotoHistorian* Supplement 109/110, 1995).

Norfolk
Cory, David, *Norwich carte de visite photographers*, in *Bygones 5*, ed. Dick Joice (Woodbridge, Boydell Press, 1980).

Northumberland
Eva, S & K, *Professional photographers in Newcastle, Gateshead and Sunderland 1873-1920* (London: RPS, *PhotoHistorian* Supplement 117, 1997).

Nottinghamshire
Heathcote, Pauline & Bernard, *Nottingham photographic studios in Victorian times 1841-1900* (London: RPS, *PhotoHistorian* Supplement 42, 1979).
Iliffe, Richard & Baguley, Wilfred, *Photography in Nottingham* in *Victorian Nottingham*, volume 16 (Nottingham: Nottingham Historical Film Unit, 1976).

Oxfordshire
Gosling, Sarah, *From Daguerre to dry plate - the growth of professional photography in Banbury 1850-1920* in *Cake & Cockhorse*, volume 9, number 6 (Banbury: Banbury Historical Society, 1987).
Smith, Mervyn L, *Professional photographers in Oxford 1842-1910* (Bath: RPS, *PhotoHistorian* Supplement 58, 1982).

Shropshire
Hallett, Michael, *Victorian and Edwardian professional photographers in Shropshire 1842-1913* (London: RPS, *PhotoHistorian* Supplement 94, 1991).
Jones, Gillian & Graham, & Hallett, Michael, *Professional photographers in Shropshire 1840-1940* (London: RPS, *PhotoHistorian* Supplement 114, 1996).

Somerset
Smith, Brian Turton, *Photographers in Bath 1841-1910* (Bath: RPS, *PhotoHistorian* Supplement 47, 1980).

Staffordshire
Jones, Gillian A, *Professional photographers in North Staffordshire 1850-1940* (London: RPS, *PhotoHistorian* Supplement 103, 1993).
Jones, Gillian A, *Professional photographers in South Staffordshire 1850-1940* (London: RPS, *PhotoHistorian* Supplement 105, 1994).

Surrey
Rimmer, Ralph W, *Professional photographers in Croydon 1860-1939* (London: RPS, *PhotoHistorian* Supplement 124, 1998).
Wilson, John, *Professional photographers in Kingston upon Thames 1854-1911* (London: RPS, *PhotoHistorian* Supplement, 1984).

Sussex
Gill, Arthur T, *Brighton photographers in Victorian times 1841-1901* (London: RPS, *PhotoHistorian* Supplement 41, 1979).
Gill, Arthur T, *Photographers in Eastbourne 1877-1910* (London: RPS, *PhotoHistorian* Supplement 65, 1984).
Gill, Arthur T, *Victorian and Edwardian photographers in Hastings, St Leonards 1852-1910 (including Bexhill)* (London: RPS, *PhotoHistorian* Supplement 73, 1986).
Grant R C & Gill, Arthur T, *Photographic studios in Victorian and Edwardian Brighton* (London: RPS, *PhotoHistorian* Supplement 116, 1997).

Warwickshire
Aston, C E John, Hallett, Michael & McKenna, Joseph, *Professional photographers in Birmingham 1842-1914* (London: RPS, *PhotoHistorian* Supplement 77, 1987).

Wiltshire
Norgate, Martin, Blades, Judith & Slocombe, Pamela, *Photographers in Wiltshire* (Trowbridge: Wiltshire Library and Museum Service, 1985).

Worcestershire
Hallett, Michael, *Professional photographers in Worcestershire 1851-1920* (London: RPS, *PhotoHistorian* Supplement 72, 1986).

Yorkshire
Adamson, Keith I P, *Commercial photographers in Doncaster 1842-1938* (Bath: RPS, *PhotoHistorian* Supplement 56, 1982).
Adamson, Keith I P, *Professional photographers in Sheffield and Rotherham 1843-1900* (Bath: RPS, *PhotoHistorian* Supplement 61, 1983).
Adamson, Keith I P, *Professional photographers in York 1844-1913* (Bath: RPS, *PhotoHistorian* Supplement, 1985).
Adamson, Keith I P, *Professional photographers in Bradford 1843-1900 (including Bingley, Shipley and Baildon)* (London: RPS, *PhotoHistorian* Supplement 96, 1992).
Adamson, Keith I P, *Professional photographers in Halifax and Huddersfield with some neighbouring towns (Sowerby Bridge, Rastrick, Brighouse, Holmfirth, Heckmondwick, Liversedge, Elland, Mirfield, Cleckheaton, Hebdon Bridge, Honley) 1843-1900* (London: RPS, *PhotoHistorian* Supplement 104, 1994).
Adamson, Keith I P, *Professional photographers on the Yorkshire coast (Withernsea to Redcar) 1842-1900* (London: RPS, *PhotoHistorian* Supplement 106, 1995).
Adamson, Keith I P & Budge, Adrian, *Professional photographers in Leeds 1842-1900* (London: RPS, *PhotoHistorian* Supplement 60, 1983).
Bayliss, Anne & Paul, *Photographers in mid-nineteenth century Scarborough: the Sarony years* (Scarborough: A M Bayliss, 1998) [SoG shelf mark: Shelf 9 (YR/LOC)].
Budge, Adrian, *Early photographers in Leeds 1839-1870* (Leeds: Leeds Art Galleries, 1981).
Elliott, Brian, *Professional photographers in the Barnsley area 1850-1940* (London: RPS, *PhotoHistorian* Supplement 121, 1998).
Murray, Hugh, *Photographs and photographers in York: the early years 1844-1879* (York: York Architectural and York Archaeological Society, 1986).
Pritchard, Michael, *Victorian and Edwardian photographers in Kingston upon Hull and Beverley1845-1911* (Bath: RPS, *PhotoHistorian* Supplement 66, 1984).

Wales

Brecknockshire
Lewis-Davies, Lin, *Photography and Powys photographers* in *Cronicl Powys* number 45 (Builth Wells: Powys FHS, December 1998) [SoG shelf mark: WS/PER].

Cardiganshire
Colboun, Megan, *Photographers in Dyfed 1857-1920* (London: RPS, *PhotoHistorian* Supplement 79, 1987).

Carmarthenshire
(See Cardiganshire).

Glamorgan
Jones, Stephen K, *The commercial camera in Cardiff 1855-1920, including Caerphilly, Cogan and Penarth* (London: RPS, *PhotoHistorian* Supplement 50, 1980).

Montgomeryshire
(See Brecknockshire.)

Pembrokeshire
(See Cardiganshire.)

Radnorshire
(See Brecknockshire.)

Scotland

There is a full series of regional directories for Scotland. The booklets are available separately, but in the library of the Society of Genealogists they have been bound together as *Photographers in Scotland to 1914*, with the shelf mark: SC/G 323.

Torrance, D Richard, *Photographers in central Scotland to 1914* (Edinburgh: Scottish Genealogy Society, 2001).
Torrance, D Richard, *Photographers in Edinburgh and the Lothians to 1914* (Edinburgh: Scottish Genealogy Society, 2001).
Torrance, D Richard, *Photographers in Lanarkshire to 1914* (Edinburgh: Scottish Genealogy Society, 2002).
Torrance, D Richard, *Photographers in north-eastern Scotland to 1914* (Edinburgh: Scottish Genealogy Society, 2001).
Torrance, D Richard, *Photographers in northern Scotland to 1914* (Edinburgh: Scottish Genealogy Society, 2001).
Torrance, D Richard, *Photographers in southern Scotland to 1914* (Edinburgh: Scottish Genealogy Society, 2001).
Torrance, D Richard, *Photographers in western Scotland to 1914* (Edinburgh: Scottish Genealogy Society, 2002).

There are also three directories that do not form part of the above series:

Lanarkshire
Hallett, Michael, *Victorian and Edwardian professional photographers in Glasgow1842-1908* (London: RPS, *PhotoHistorian* Supplement, 1990).

Midlothian
Stubbs, Peter, *Professional photographers in Edinburgh, Leith and Portobello 1840-1940* (London: RPS, *PhotoHistorian* Supplement 135/136, 2001).

Renfrewshire
McCoo, Donald, *Paisley photographers 1850-1900* (Glasgow: Foulis Archive Press, 1986).

Northern Ireland

Maguire, W A, *A century in focus: photography and photographers in the North of Ireland 1839-1939* (Belfast: Blackstaff, 2000).

2. Online directories

A number of photographer directories have now been placed online, and it is to be expected that the trend will continue. Photographer directories are not obviously attractive commercial propositions for traditional publishers, but they do seem to attract a healthy level of user attention when they take the form of websites. Some of the sites are noticeably less thorough than others, but they are included in the following list. Researchers will use their own judgement when consulting them. There also exist one or two lists based simply on a single trade directory or on studios represented in an individual's collection of old photographs. These are not included.

On a more positive note, some of these sites are more than mere directories and have much additional information on studios and photographers. It can therefore be worth exploring a site as a whole, rather than just extracting one or two dates and addresses.

England *(mainland)*

Cambridgeshire
Pols, Robert, *Early photographic studios: a directory of early studio photographers in Cambridgeshire* | www.early-photographers.org.uk

Cheshire
Holland, Paul, *Victorian and Edwardian photographers (Chester and north-east Wales).*
www.hollandfamilyhistory.co.uk/htmlfiles/victorianphotographers.html

Cleveland
Cleveland, North Yorkshire and South Durham Family History Society, *Cleveland Family History Society: photographers in the area.*
www.clevelandfhs.org.uk/Photographers.htm

Derbyshire
Payne, Brett, *An Index to Derbyshire Photographers & Photographic Studios.*
http://freepages.genealogy.rootsweb.ancestry.com/~brett/photos/dbyphoto_index.html

Gloucestershire
Vaughan, Roger, *Bristol photographers UK (1852-1972).*
www.cartes.fsnet.co.uk/photo/azlist2.htm

Hampshire
Pomeroy, Stephen, *Portsmouth photographers.*
http://homepage.ntlworld.com/stephen.pomeroy/local/photo.pdf

Lancashire
Anonymous, *Liverpool photographers.*
http://freepages.genealogy.rootsweb.ancestry.com/~liverpoolphotographers

London
Webb, David, *photoLondon* | www.photolondon.org.uk/default.asp

Norfolk
Pols, Robert, *Early photographic studios: a directory of early studio photographers in Norfolk* | www.early-photographers.org.uk

Oxfordshire
Gosling, Sarah, *From Daguerre to dry plate - the growth of professional photography in Banbury 1850-1920.*
www.cherwell.gov.uk/media/pdf/b/4/pdf8182386799191835067.PDF#search=%22Please%20enter%20a%20keyword%22

Staffordshire
Harbach, Mike, *Staffordshire photographers index.*
www.genuki.org.uk/big/eng/STS/Stsphots.html

Suffolk
Pols, Robert, *Early photographic studios: a directory of early studio photographers in Suffolk* | www.early-photographers.org.uk

Sussex
Simkin, David, *Directory of photographic studios in Brighton and Hove 1841-1910.* www.spartacus.schoolnet.co.uk/DSindex.htm
Simkin, David, *Sussex PhotoHistory* | www.photohistory-sussex.co.uk/index.htm

Warwickshire
Trepess, Pickard, *Victorian photography studios (in Birmingham and Warwickshire)* | http://www.hunimex.com/warwick/photogs.html

Wales

(Coverage is national in one instance and regional in another, so organisation by county has, in this section, been abandoned).

Alderman, Mari, *Victorian professional photographers in Wales 1850-1925.*
www.genuki.org.uk/big/wal/VicPhoto1.html
Holland, Paul, *Victorian and Edwardian photographers (Chester and north-east Wales)*
www.hollandfamilyhistory.co.uk/htmlfiles/victorianphotographers.html
Meazey, Peter, *Glamorgan photographers.*
www.genuki.org.uk/big/wal/GLA/Photographers.html
Smosarski, Albie, *History of the postcard and Tenby photographers.*
www.visittenby.co.uk/history/hptp

Scotland

Ayrshire
Close, Rob, *Nineteenth century photographers in Ayrshire: a preliminary list.*
www.ayrshirehistory.org.uk/Photographers/photographers1.htm

Fife
Fife Family History Society, *Fife photographers to 1900.*
www.fifefhs.org/Records/photographers.htm

Lanarkshire
Low, Arthur, *Glasgow's Victorian photographers.*
www.thelows.madasafish.com/main.htm#mid

Midlothian
Stubbs, Peter, *Edinburgh's professional photographers.*
www.edinphoto.org.uk/2/2__professional_photographers.htm

Islands

Jersey
Hemery, Richard, *Jersey photographers and studios.*
http://jerseyfamilyhistory.co.uk/?page_id=11

Isle of Man
Coakley, Frances, *Manx note book: photographers.*
www.isle-of-man.com/manxnotebook/tourism/pgrphrs/pgrhrs.htm

Isle of Wight
Childs, Gordon, *Isle of Wight photographers* | www.iowphotos.info

3. Photographic chains

A few photographic businesses developed into chains on a regional or national scale. Individual branches should be found in the directory (if there is one) for their locality, but some limited help is available - in print or online - to researchers wishing to investigate the whole chain. As with its Supplements so with the journal itself, *The PhotoHistorian*'s primary location of publication is listed in the British Library catalogue as London rather than Bath. This practice has been followed both here and elsewhere in the book.

Directories in print:

Linkman, Audrey, *The photographic multiple in the nineteenth century* in *The PhotoHistorian*, number 110 (London: RPS, January 1996).
Linkman, Audrey, *Brown, Barnes and Bell* in *The PhotoHistorian*, number 111 (London: RPS, March 1996).
Osman, Colin, *The studios of A & G Taylor* (London: RPS, PhotoHistorian Supplement 111, 1996).

Directory online:

Vaughan, Roger, *The studios of A & G Taylor (Andrew and George Taylor).*
http://homepages.tesco.net/~roger.vaughan/visitors/taylor-ag.htm

4. Online pay-per-view directories

Two UK websites offer directory-style information for a fee. The drawback of such services is their precise focus. There is no provision for browsing an area's directory to identify earlier and later occupants of a studio, or to see whether a studio was in a street that was popular with photographers. But where there is no other directory for a locality, or where a printed directory proves difficult to obtain, these sites have an obvious attraction. Their fees are modest.

Index of UK portrait & studio photographers c1840-1950
www.earlyphotographers.org.uk/welcome.html
Rosemary and Stan Rodliffe's site refers searchers to printed and online directories where they exist. But they have also compiled their own directories - some of them to areas not otherwise covered - and these can be searched for a fee. Whilst some of their directories draw on a wide range of sources, others are less thorough. In the case of Wales, for instance, information dates (at the time of writing) from 1881, 1884, 1910 and 1920. But the scope of a database is generally indicated, so researchers can judge for themselves whether it is worth submitting a query. The site's many links include a useful selection of photographer biographies.

Photographers of Great Britain and Ireland 1840-1949
www.cartedevisite.co.uk
This site, the work of Ron Cosens, offers information on (at the time of writing) 33,000 photographers and over 62,000 studio addresses. It draws information from census returns as well as trade directories, and it gives users the opportunity to see what kind of information is available about a given photographer before making a decision to buy. (Researchers wishing to proceed straight to the search-and-purchase area of the site should go to www.victorianphotographers.co.uk.) There is also a growing number of biographies, to which access is free, and new features of interest are promised for the future. Already of considerable potential value, the site is worth revisiting periodically, to check how it develops.

CHAPTER FOUR
Material in archives

The researcher's dream is to discover a full set of studio records that documents a photographer's day-to-day business; the waking reality almost always falls far short of that. Where archived collections exist, they are most likely to be of negatives or prints with little accompanying information. Any additional records are a rare bonus. But the images that such collections preserve are valuable in themselves. They offer insight into the photographer's range of activities, markets and skills, and most investigators will consider them worth seeking out, regardless of how little extra information comes with them.

When a collection of interest is identified, however, it's important to check precisely what is available for inspection, and under what conditions. To turn up at a repository expecting immediate access to the desired items is to invite disappointment. Arrangements vary from institution to institution, but appointments may be necessary and, increasingly, researchers are being encouraged to study digitised images (often online) rather than glass negatives or original prints. In some cases, negatives are kept off-site, sometimes in frozen storage.

The basic contact information that's given for repositories in the following pages may help to initiate the preliminary checking.

1. National Collections

In 1987 twelve photographic collections were identified as having national importance. The years since then have seen some organisational name-changes and one major migration of holdings, but the collections in question provide a useful starting point for a review of photographic archives. Indeed, they are probably too important to be ignored. They do, however, vary greatly in their potential usefulness to those studying individual studio photographers.

The National Archives
Kew, Richmond, Surrey, TW9 4DU | Tel: 020 8876 3444.
www.nationalarchives.gov.uk

Whilst the photographic material held at The National Archive comprises millions of individual items, it is not focused on studio photographers, there are no specific collections relating to individual practitioners, and only a small percentage of the photographs have been identified and catalogued. Many items have been kept to complement other documentary material rather than because they are seen as significant in their own right.

There may, however, be material of interest to some researchers in the COPY series of records. These relate to applications for registration of proprietorship at Stationers' Hall, under the Copyright Acts governing the period 1842-1912. The original forms of application have been preserved and they are generally accompanied by copies of the images that their creators sought to protect. The names of 'authors' of photographs and of copyright holders that appear within the COPY1 series have been added to The National Archives' online catalogue.

Researchers wishing to investigate the holdings at The National Archives are advised to study the online In-depth Research Guides - *Photographs for Research* and *Photographic Series in The National Archives (introduction and inventory lists)*. Both guides can be downloaded from the website: www.nationalarchives.gov.uk/records/research-guide-listing.htm#p.

The British Library
96 Euston Road, London, NW1 2DB | Tel: 020 7412 7676.
www.bl.uk

Except in the case of eminent practitioners, the collection has tended to be subject-driven rather than photographer-driven, but the work of some studio photographers is included in the holdings. There are catalogues of photographs, photographically illustrated books and texts relating to photography, and a project funded by the Jerwood Charitable Foundation is currently in the process of making these available online at www.bl.uk/catalogues/photographs.

The value of British Library catalogues for locating printed works as well as images should not, of course, be overlooked.

The National Portrait Gallery
St Martin's Place, London, WC2 0HE | Tel: 020 7306 0055.
www.npg.org.uk/collections/about/photographs-collection.php

The Photographs Collection is made up of more than 220,000 images. Many of the photographers represented are relatively modern, and many fall outside the definition of studio photographer. But high street practitioners are also included, and there are major holdings related to:

Bassano, Alexander	Beresford, George
Edis, Olive	Elliott & Fry
Foulsham & Banfield	Hollyer, Frederick
Lafayette, James	Maull & Polyblank
(real name: Lauder, James)	
Mayall, John (and sons)	Silvy, Camille
Stoneman, Walter	Vandyk, Carl
Watkins, Herbert	

The work of some studio photographers is also included in the Sydney Buxton, Earl Buxton collection. Other professionals represented in the collection can be identified using the A-Z guide on the website.

Researchers wishing to see images that are not on display in the main gallery are asked to contact the Curator of Photographs in writing.

The Scottish National Photography Collection
The Scottish National Portrait Gallery, 1 Queen Street, Edinburgh, EH2 1JD.
Tel: 0131 624 6200 | www.nationalgalleries.org/portraitgallery

Scottish photographers, both professional and amateur, are well represented in this collection, and there are significant holdings of pictures (and some business documents) by such practitioners as George Washington Wilson, John Moffat and Thomas Annan. The collection is not, however, confined to Scottish photographs.

Unfortunately, at the time of writing, the gallery is closed for a major refurbishment project and its research resources are unavailable. A much-improved gallery, with a stronger emphasis on photography, is due to open at the end of 2011. Meanwhile an introduction to the collections and biographical notes on a range of photographers can be found in:

> Stevenson, Sara, & Forbes, Duncan, *Companion Guide to Photography in the National Galleries of Scotland* (Edinburgh: National Galleries of Scotland, 1990)

The National Library of Wales
Penglais, Aberystwyth, Ceredigion, SY23 3BU | Tel: 01970 632 800.
www.llgc.org.uk

The Library houses over 800,000 photographs connected to Wales. Of these, some 35,000 are Welsh views taken by Francis Frith's company, and another 3,000 are the work of John Thomas. P B Abery, D C Harries, William Harwood and Arthur Lewis are among the more studio-focused professionals who are well represented. An online catalogue can be used to search the holdings.

The Victoria & Albert Museum
Cromwell Road, South Kensington, London, SW7 2RL | Tel: 020 7942 2000.
www.vam.ac.uk

There is a photography gallery, focusing on the history of photography, but very few pictures are on display at any one time. The collection, however, runs to around 500,000 images, and there are significant holdings relating to studio photographers W & D Downey, Frederick Hollyer and James Lafayette (James Lauder). The collection can be searched online by photographers' names at http://collections.vam.ac.uk.

The National Monuments Record Centre
Kerrible Drive, Churchward Village, Swindon, SN2 2GZ | Tel: 01793 414600.
www.english-heritage.org.uk/daysout/properties/national-monuments-record-centre

The focus of the photographic collection is England's historic environment, so any light it can shed on the work of individual photographers is purely incidental. Notable early contributors to the record were architectural specialists Bedford Lemere & Co and studio photographer Henry Taunt.

The Imperial War Museum
Lambeth Road, London, SE1 6HZ | Tel: 020 7416 5320 | www.iwm.org.uk

Here, too, it is subject rather than photographer that is important. But the museum holds nearly 11 million photographs, some of which were taken by photographers who spent at least part of their careers in the studio. The website's search engine (at www.iwmcollections.org.uk/qryPhotoImg.php) allows researchers to check whether a particular photographer is represented.

The Tate Gallery
Millbank, London, SW1P 4RG | Tel: 020 7887 8888 | www.tate.org.uk

Though the Tate archive holds about 100,000 photographic images, its concern with photography is primarily within the context of fine art practice. Studio photographers are not likely to be found, but the website has a search facility that allows researchers to check for themselves.

Birmingham Central Library
Chamberlain Square, Birmingham, B3 3HQ | Tel: 0121 303 4511.
www.birmingham.gov.uk/centrallibrary

The library's extensive photographic holdings have a strong local dimension. There are major collections relating to Harold Baker, Francis Bedford and Ernest Dyche, and other local studio photographers are represented in the Photographic Portraits Collection (for which an index is available).

Bearing in mind that organised photographic groups often had both amateur and professional members, it's also worth noting that the library has records of the Birmingham Photographic Society and the Midland Counties Photographic Federation. Records of the British Institute of Professional Photographers (founded in 1901, and originally known as the Professional Photographers' Association) have also been deposited, but no arrangement for public access is likely to be considered until after a projected move to new premises in - probably - 2013.

A dated (but not entirely obsolete) overview of holdings is provided by *Coming Into Light: Birmingham Central Library's Photographic Collections* by Peter James in *PhotoResearcher* number 6, March 1977. This can be found online at www.donau-uni.ac.at/en/department/bildwissenschaft/partnerlinks/eshph/09767/index.php. (More information about *PhotoResearcher* is given in the chapter 'Periodicals and serial publications'.)

The Royal Photographic Society
Fenton House, 122 Wells Road, Bath, BA2 3AH | Tel: 01225 325733.
www.rps.org

The contact details above may be of use for those wishing to find out more about the society, but its collection of equipment, photographs and other documents has now been transferred to the care of the National Media Museum.

The collection is particularly strong in its coverage of photographic pioneers and early techniques, which inevitably means some emphasis on the gentleman amateur rather than the high street professional. But the varied documents include letters, catalogues and drafts of speeches, and there are more than two hundred minute books relating to various Society proceedings.

Researchers could better assess the potential value of these records if they knew whether (and when) a photographic ancestor belonged to the RPS. Help is imminent. Michael Pritchard has reached the final stages of a project to compile a database of RPS members from 1853 to 1900. This database, which will be searchable and freely available, is expected to be ready before the end of 2011. There is also a possibility that it will eventually be extended to cover the period 1901-1920. More information should become available in due course at www.mpritchard.com or http://britishphotohistory.ning.com.

The National Media Museum
Bradford, West Yorkshire, BD1 1NQ | Tel: 0844 856 3797.
www.nationalmediamuseum.org.uk

The photography collection would be difficult to match for its diversity. It is, in effect, a collection of collections, since it now houses those of the Science Museum, the Kodak Museum, the Daily Herald Archive and the Royal Photographic Society.

The museum's Collections and Research Centre, Insight, has a suite of research rooms and can provide access to over 3.2 million images. Its archives of printed material house books, periodicals, trade literature and ephemera, and it is the home of the Royal Photographic Society's library. There are, however, no collections relating to individual photographers or studios. Appointments can be made by ringing 0870 7010 200.

It should be noted that the website's search facility covers only the website: it does not locate holdings.

2. Other repositories: single-studio collections

The collections listed in this section relate to the work of a single photographer, family of photographers or studio. Some exist as discrete collections, but others are substantial single-studio holdings within a larger collection. They are listed in alphabetical order of photographer and include repository contact details and brief descriptive notes.

Alger, Cleer
Ipswich Record Office, Gatacre Road, Ipswich, Suffolk, IP1 2LQ.
Tel: 01473 584541 | www.suffolk.gov.uk/sro

A collection of about 600 glass plate negatives from two generations of Diss photographers.

Annan, Thomas
The Mitchell Library, North Street, Glasgow, G3 7DN | Tel: 0141 287 29999 or 0141 287 2876 | www.glasgow.gov.uk/en/Residents/Library_Services/The_Mitchell

A collection of over 500 photographs of nineteenth century Glasgow and the surrounding area.

Ashley, George & Abraham
The Armitt Collection, Rydal Road, Ambleside, Cumbria, LA22 9BL.
Tel: 01539 431212 | http://armitt.com/armitt_collection.htm

The Ashleys are among a number of local photographers whose work can be found in the photographic section of the collection, and who are profiled on the website. (Others are Herbert Bell, J W Brunskill, and Charles Walmsley.)

Bagshaw, Luke
Doncaster Archives Department, King Edward Road, Balby, Doncaster, DN4 0NA.
Tel: 01302 859811 | www.doncaster.gov.uk/Leisure_in_Doncaster/Libraries/Archives_Local_Studies/Doncaster_Archives.asp

A collection of account books, receipt books, receipted invoices, correspondence and more relating to the business of Bagshaw and Son, The earliest items date from about 1882, but most fall between 1892 and 1930.

Bale, Stewart
Maritime Archives & Library, Merseyside Maritime Museum, Albert Dock, Liverpool, L3 4AQ | Tel: 0151 478 4499.
www.liverpoolmuseums.org.uk/maritime/archive/

This is a vast collection of over 195,000 negatives (glass and film) from a commercial studio that specialised in industrial photography. Though the company was established in about 1911, the images date from the 1920s and later. There are also some negative registers and client registers. The collection is stored off-site, so preliminary contact is vital.

Balmain, James C H
Edinburgh Room, Edinburgh Central Library. 9 George IV Bridge, Edinburgh, EH1 1EG | Tel: 0131 242 8030.
www.edinburgh.gov.uk/directory_record/5083/edinburgh_room

A collection of photographs dating mainly from the period 1900-1920.

Bassano & Vandyk
Museum of London, 150 London Wall, London, EC2Y 5HN | Tel: 020 7001 9844.
www.museumoflondon.org.uk/English/Collections/1700Today/Photographs.htm

Over 3,000 glass negatives of fashion advertisements from 1913 onward.

Baudoux, Ernest
Photographic Archive, The Société Jersiaise, 7 Pier Road, St Helier, Jersey, JE2 4XW. Tel: 01534 758314 | www.societe-jersiaise.org/photographic-archive/about-the-photographic-archive.html.

Baudoux (active c1869-1894) is just one of the photographers whose work forms a substantial presence in the extensive collection of the Société Jersiaise. Amateurs are also included, and there are a number of professionals who are represented by only a handful of images. But, as well as for Baudoux, there are significant holdings for William Collie, Percival Dunham, Francis Foot, Henry Mullins, Clarence Ouless, Albert Smith and Frederick Spinner.

Begbie, Thomas
City Art Centre, Address: 2 Market Street, Edinburgh, EH1 1DE | Tel: 0131 529 3993.
http://www.edinburgh.gov.uk/internet/leisure/museums_and_galleries/CEC_city_art_centre

A collection of glass negatives by an amateur-turned professional, whose photographic activity began in the 1850s.

Bell, Herbert
See Ashley, above.

Bevan, Henry William
Lowestoft Record Office, Clapham Road Lowestoft, Suffolk, NR32 1DR.
Tel: 01502 405357 | www.suffolk.gov.uk/sro

One of three Lowestoft photographers represented by a glass negative collection stretching from the 1870s into the first half of the twentieth century. (The other photographers are Charles Metcalf and Christopher Wilson.)

Blanchard, Valentine
See Clarke, below.

Bliss, J E
See Clarke, below.

Bolas, S B
City of Westminster Archives Centre, 10 St Ann's Street, London, SW1P 2DE.
Tel: 020 7641 5180 | www.westminster.gov.uk/services/libraries/archives

A group of photographs, rather than a discrete collection, by a noted architectural photographer.

Bool, Alfred & John
Museum of London, 150 London Wall, London, EC2Y 5HN | Tel: 020 7001 9844.
www.museumoflondon.org.uk/English/Collections/1700Today/Photographs.htm

Photographs of historic London buildings, 1870s/1880s.

Bourne, Frederick
East Sussex Record Office, The Maltings, Castle Precinct, Lewes, BN7 1YT.
Tel: 01273 482349 | http://www.eastsussex.gov.uk/leisureandtourism/
localandfamilyhistory/esro

Glass negatives of an Eastbourne photographer, c1890-1839.

Braddock, Alfred
Hackney Archives, 43 De Beauvoir Road, N1 5SQ | Tel: 020 7241 2886.
www.hackney.gov.uk/ca-archives-collections.htm

Two large groups of Braddock's negatives - one of which was rescued from a skip - have now been reintegrated into a single collection (c1884-1907).

Brunskill, J W
See Ashley, above.

Bustin, Richard, Marion & William Henry
Herefordshire Record Office, Harold Street, Hereford HR1 2QX | Tel: 01432 260750.
www.herefordshire.gov.uk/leisure/archives/3584.asp

A large collection of glass plate negatives from a Hereford family business.

Chapman, J T
Museum of Science & Industry, Liverpool Road, Castlefield, Manchester, M3 4FP.
Tel: 0161 832 2244 | http://www.mosi.org.uk/collections.aspx

A collection of dry plate negatives and photographic equipment

Clarke, J Palmer
Cambridge Central Library, 7 Lion Yard, Cambridge, CB2 3QD | Tel: 0345 045 5225.
www.cambridgeshire.gov.uk/leisure/archives/local_history/cambs/photographs_and_illustrations.htm

Clarke is one of the photographers represented in the J Palmer Clarke/Ramsey & Muspratt Portrait Collection, which includes an archive of over 50,000 glass plate negatives of portraits taken during his time at Post Office Terrace, Cambridge, between the 1890s and the 1930s. But Clarke was not the first photographer to use the studio, and every time the business changed hands, the negative collection passed on. So the archive of images continued to grow under his successors. Two of these, Lettice Ramsay and Helen Muspratt, built an international reputation and are also commemorated in the title of the collection. The complete collection runs to well over a quarter of a million images and covers the years from the 1860s to the 1980s.

In chronological order, the photographers at the Post Office Terrace studio were: Arthur Nicholls, J E Bliss, Valentine Blanchard, Colin Lunn, John Palmer Clarke, C E Goodrich & F Sanderson, Lettice Ramsay & Helen Muspratt, Nicholas Lee, Peter Lofts.

See also The Cambridgeshire Collection in the 'Online Archives' section later in this chapter.

Collie, William
See Baudoux, above.

Corin, Walter
Surrey History Centre, 130 Goldsworth Road, Woking, Surrey, GU21 6ND.
Tel: 01483 518737 | www.surreycc.gov.uk/sccwebsite/sccwspages.nsf/
LookupWebPagesByTITLE_RTF/Surrey+History+Centre?opendocument

A series of autochrome photographs dated c1910-1912.

Cowell
Ipswich Record Office, Gatacre Road, Ipswich, Suffolk, IP1 2LQ | Tel: 01473 584541.
www.suffolk.gov.uk/sro

About 1,500 glass negatives from an Ipswich postcard publisher. Most date from 1905-1908, but a few are later.

Dixon, Henry
Museum of London, 150 London Wall, London, EC2Y 5HN | Tel: 020 7001 9844.
www.museumoflondon.org.uk/English/Collections/1700Today/Photographs.htm

Photographs of historic London buildings, 1870s/1880s.

Doran family
Whitby Museum, Pannett Park, Whitby, North Yorkshire, YO21 1RE.
Tel: 01947 602908 | www.whitbymuseum.org.uk/d12/photo/index.htm

The Doran studio opened for business in 1905, but most photographs in this collection date from later generations of the family.

Doull, David
Edinburgh Room, Edinburgh Central Library, 9 George IV Bridge,
Edinburgh, EH1 1EG | Tel: 0131 242 8030.
www.edinburgh.gov.uk/directory_record/5083/edinburgh_room

A collection of over 300 glass negatives dating from the 1860s.

Dunham, Percival
See Baudoux, above.

Eason, Arthur
Hackney Museum, Ground Floor, Technology and Learning Centre, 1 Reading Lane, E8 1GQ | Tel: 020 8356 3500 | www.hackney.gov.uk/cm-museum.htm

A collection of studio photographs, c1880-1890.

Edis, Olive
Cromer Museum, East Cottages, Tucker Street, Cromer, Norfolk, NR27 9HB.
Tel: 01263 513543 | www.museums.norfolk.gov.uk/Visit_Us/Cromer_Museum/index.htm

The Cyril Nunn Collection of Edis' work is made up of prints, glass negatives and, unusually, a number of autochromes.

Fisher, Walter
Filey Museum, 8/10 Queen Street, Filey, North Yorkshire, YO14 9HB.
Tel: 01723 515013 | www.fileymuseum.co.uk/filey_museum_room8.htm

A collection of photographs is currently being catalogued by volunteers. The telephone is manned only during the limited opening hours of this museum, which is staffed entirely by volunteers.

Flather, Henry
Museum of London, 150 London Wall, London, EC2Y 5HN.
Tel: 020 7001 9844 | www.museumoflondon.org.uk/English/Collections/1700Today/Photographs.htm

Photographs of the construction of the Metropolitan and District Railway, 1860s.

Foot, Francis
See Baudoux, above.

Fowke, Charles Edward
Staffordshire Record Office, Eastgate Street, Stafford, ST16 2LZ | Tel: 01785 278379.
www.staffordshire.gov.uk/leisure/archives/contact/sro

Around 2,000 glass plates make up a collection covering the period c1890-1930, though most date from 1900-1920. It is possible that some of the negatives originate from Fowke's partnership with Paul Weiss (1905-1915), and some may date from H H Tilley's earlier occupancy of Fowke's Stafford studio.

Freeman, William Philip Barnes
Norfolk Record Office, The Archive Centre, Martineau Lane, Norwich, NR1 2DQ.
Tel: 01603 222599 | www.archives.norfolk.gov.uk/nroindex.htm

The collection relating to this Norwich photographer and artist includes letters and other papers dating from the 1830s to the 1890s.

Frith, Francis

Local and regional holdings of Frith photographs are not uncommon. Some - as at the National Library of Wales, the Hampshire Record Office, the Armitt Collection and the Suffolk Record Office, Bury St Edmunds - take the form of readily identifiable collections. Others may be found by investigating general topographical collections.

See also the 'Online Archives' section later in this chapter.

Goodrich, C E
See Clarke, above.

Graham, William
The Mitchell Library, North Street, Glasgow, G3 7DN. | Tel: 0141 287 29999 or 0141 287 2876 | www.glasgow.gov.uk/en/Residents/Library_Services/The_Mitchell

A significant holding of Graham's photographs forms part of the library's Glasgow Collection.

Hardman, Edward Chambré
Liverpool Record Office, Central Library, William Brown Street, Liverpool, L3 8EW | Tel: 0151 233 3000 or 0151 233 5835 | www.liverpool.gov.uk/archives

Hardman's photographic activity had begun by 1912, but he did not establish his first studio until the 1920s. The earliest photographs in this collection date from about 1916.

Researchers should note that temporary arrangements for (possibly limited) access to archives will apply until some time in 2012. Contact details will change with the move to new premises.

Hardman, Joseph
Cumbria Record Office, Kendal County Offices, Kendal, LA9 4RQ.
Tel: 01539 713540 or 01539 713539.
www.cumbria.gov.uk/archives/recordoffices/knrec.asp)

A mixed collection of photographs, notes, family albums and business correspondence, c1910-1970.

Hickox, Herbert Edward
Surrey History Centre, 130 Goldsworth Road, Woking, Surrey, GU21 6ND.
Tel: 01483 518737 | www.surreycc.gov.uk/sccwebsite/sccwspages.nsf/
LookupWebPagesByTITLE_RTF/Surrey+History+Centre?opendocument

Photographs by, and a biography of, a Wimbledon photographer and photographic inventor.

Hollyer, Frederick
Glasgow School of Art, 167 Renfrew Street, Glasgow, G3 6RQ | Tel: 0141 353 4500.
www.gsa.ac.uk/gsa.cfm?pid=1859

Some photographs by Hollyer are included in an album along with photographs by Guido Rey and drawings by Edward Burne-Jones.

Jackson, Magnus
Perth Museum & Art Gallery, George street, Perth, PH7 3NF | Tel: 01738 632488.
www.pkc.gov.uk/Education+and+learning/Museums+and+galleries/Perth+Museum+and+Art+Gallery/Collections/Photographic+Collection

A collection of around 2,500 glass negatives.

Jarman, Harry Isaac
Bury Record Office, 77 Raingate Street, Bury St Edmunds, Suffolk, IP33 2AR.
Tel: 01284 35235 | www.suffolk.gov.uk/sro

In 1901 Jarman bought the business and negatives of two generations of Spanton (William and William Silas). The Spanton-Jarman collection of about 4,000 glass negatives preserves the work of all three photographers and covers a period from the 1860s to the 1940s.

Kent, Tom
Orkney Library & Archive, 44 Junction Road, Kirkwall, Orkney, KW15 1AG.
Tel: 01856 873166 | www.orkneylibrary.org.uk/html/photographers.htm

Over 200 of Kent's photographs are preserved in the Orkney Photographic Archive.

Kevis, Walter
West Sussex Record Office, 3 Orchard Street, Chichester, West Sussex, PO19 1DD.
Tel: 01243 753602 | www.westsussex.gov.uk/leisure/explore_west_sussex/record_office_and_archives/about_us_location_opening_ho.aspx

About 5,000 negatives. Around 500 are views of the Petworth area, and the rest are portraits, for many of which the date, sitter and location are recorded. All the portraits have been indexed, and the index is searchable partly online and partly on cards at Orchard Street. Access to the original glass plates is not normally permitted, but prints can be supplied.

Although the repository is at Orchard Street, the correspondence address is County Archivist, West Sussex Record Office, County Hall, Chichester, West Sussex, PO19 1RN.

Knights-Whittome, David
Sutton Local Studies and Archives Centre, St Nicholas Way, Sutton, Surrey, SM1 1EA.
Tel: 020 8770 4777 | www.sutton.gov.uk/index.aspx?articleid=1883

The collection consists of a series of ledger books, 1888-1903.

Lafayette Ltd (Manchester studio)
Greater Manchester County Record Office, 56 Marshall Street, New Cross, Manchester | Tel: 0161 832 5284 | www.gmcro.co.uk

The studio was established in the early 1890s, but this collection of half-plate negatives dates from 1927 and later.

Lance, Frank
Stockport Central Heritage Library, Wellington Road South, Stockport, SK1 3RS.
Tel: 0161 474 4530 | www.stockport.gov.uk/services/leisureculture/libraries/yourlibrary/yourlocallibrary/centralheritagelibrary2

Over 100 photographs by Lance, taken in 1900 and 1901, form part of the Stockport Photographic Society archive.

Lemere, Harry Bedford
City of Westminster Archives Centre, 10 St Ann's Street, London, SW1P 2DE.
Tel: 020 7641 5180 | www.westminster.gov.uk/services/libraries/archives

A group of photographs, rather than a discrete collection, by a noted architectural photographer.

Lunn, Colin
See Clarke, above.

Mallinson, J
Shropshire Archives, Shropshire Council, Community Services, Castle Gates, Shrewsbury, Shropshire, SY2 6ND | Tel: 01743 255350.
www.shropshire.gov.uk/archives.nsf

A series of items relating to a Frankwell photographer. The earliest date from 1919, but most are later (up to 1952).

Maull, Henry (including Maull & Co, Maull & Polyblank and Maull & Fox)
1. Library and Information Services, The Royal Society, 6-9 Carlton House Terrace, London, SW1Y 5AG | Tel: 020 7451 2606 | http://royalsociety.org/Maull-Portrait-Photograph-Collection/

A collection based on the portraits of Fellows that Maull was contracted to take from the mid-nineteenth century until the early twentieth century. An article on the collection, by Christine Woollett, can be downloaded from the website.

2. London Metropolitan Archives, 40 Northampton Road, Clerkenwell, London, EC1R 0HB | Tel: 020 7332 3820 | http://search.lma.gov.uk/OPAC_LMA/login.html

Four albums of portraits of councilmen, 1868. The need to make an appointment is emphasised.

Metcalf, Charles
See Bevan, above.

Moss, William Dennis
Gloucestershire Archives, Clarence Row, Alvin Street, Gloucester, GL1 3DW.
Tel: 01452 425295 | www.gloucestershire.gov.uk/archives

Items relating to Moss are a small part of a collection from the Abbey Studios, Cirencester. Most of the material is modern, but some documents from the studio's earliest days have survived. Other (mostly later) photographers represented in the collection are F Mortimer Savory, George Roper, Edward Parrott, Peter Reason, Graham Light and Chris Bowler.

Mullins, Henry
See Baudoux, above.

Muspratt, Helen
See Clarke, above. (Examples of Ramsey & Muspratt images can also be found at www.loftyimages.co.uk and at www.cromwellcollection.org.uk/cambscoll/airmen.html.

Nicholls, Arthur
See Clarke, above.
(Some examples of his work can be found at www.loftyimages.co.uk.)

Ouless, Clarence Philip
See Baudoux, above.

Payne, Edward Nixon & Jack Newsam
Essex Record Office, Wharf Road, Chelmsford, CM2 6YT | Tel: 01245 244644.
www.essex.gov.uk/Libraries-Archives/Record-Office/Pages/Record-Office.aspx

A collection of glass negatives, some from the late nineteenth century, and a wooden contact-printing frame.

Plowright, Walter Cole
Norfolk Record Office, The Archive Centre, Martineau Lane, Norwich, NR1 2DQ. Tel: 01603 222599 | www.archives.norfolk.gov.uk/nroindex.htm

Some papers of a Swaffham photographer from the period 1865-1911.

Ramsey, Lettice
See Clarke, above.(Examples of Ramsey & Muspratt images can also be found at www.loftyimages.co.uk and at www.cromwellcollection.org.uk/cambscoll/airmen.html.)

Ream, Lilian
Wisbech Library, Ely Place, Wisbech, PE13 1EU | Tel: 0345 045 5225.
www.cambridgeshire.gov.uk/leisure/archives/local_history/lilianream

An extensive collection of photographs covering the period 1907-1971, with an online catalogue covering around 2,500 items. (The original negatives are in the care of the Lilian Ream Exhibition Gallery Trust, for which see the 'Online Archives' section later in this chapter.)

Roberts, Thomas and Henry (Rousham Roberts)
Radnorshire Museum, Temple Street, Llandrindod Wells, Powys, LD1 5DL.
Tel: 01597 824513 | www.powys.gov.uk/index.php?id=2118&L=0

A collection of some 2,000 glass negatives from the studio of Thomas Roberts and his son Henry. The business used a family middle name and came to be known as Rousham Roberts.

Rodger, Thomas
Department of Special Collections, University of St Andrews Library, North Street, St Andrews, Fife, KY16 9TR | Tel: 01334 462339.
http://special.st-andrews.ac.uk/saspecial

A Scottish pioneer, a selection of whose work forms part of the library's Early Photographs collection.

Salmon, Sidney C
The Corstorphine Heritage Centre, The Dower House, St Margaret's Park, Edinburgh, EH12 7SX | Tel: 0131 316 4246 | www.corstorphine-trust.ukgo.com/index.html

The Trust holds a collection of Salmon's photographs from the late nineteenth and early twentieth centuries and features a profile of him on its website.

Sanderson, F
See Clarke, above.

Savory, F M
Gloucestershire Archives, Clarence Row, Alvin Street, Gloucester, GL1 3DW.
Tel: 01452 425295; www.gloucestershire.gov.uk/archives

Items relating to Savory are a small part of a collection from the Abbey Studios, Cirencester. Most of the material is modern, but some documents from the studio's earliest days have survived. Other (mostly later) photographers represented in the collection are William Moss, George Roper, Edward Parrott, Peter Reason, Graham Light and Chris Bowler.

Shaw, John William & Alfred
Blackburn Museum and Art Gallery, Museum Street, Blackburn, BB1 7AJ.
Tel: 01254 667130 | www.cottontown.org/page.cfm?pageid=2814&language=eng

A collection of glass negatives from two generations of a family business.

Smith, Albert
See Baudoux, above.

Smith, Sarah & Percy
Ipswich Record Office, Gatacre Road, Ipswich, Suffolk, IP1 2LQ.
Tel: 01473 584541 | www.suffolk.gov.uk/sro

Over 300 postcard views from the Smith's Suitall series, c1904-1910.

Spalding, Fred & family
Essex Record Office, Wharf Road, Chelmsford, CM2 6YT | Tel: 01245 244644.
www.essex.gov.uk/Libraries-Archives/Record-Office/Pages/Record-Office.aspx

The Spalding records form part of a varied collection of Chelmsford papers. There is also a separate typescript biography of Fred Spalding by Stanley M Jarvis.

Spanton, William
See Jarman, above.

Speight, James
Warwickshire County Record Office, Priory Park, Cape Road, Warwick, CV34 4JS.
Tel: 01926 738959 | www.warwickshire.gov.uk/countyrecordoffice

A diary, spread over several exercise books, kept by the youngest member of a Rugby family of photographers.

Spinner, Frederick William
See Baudoux, above.

Sutcliffe, Frank Meadow
Whitby Museum, Pannett Park, Whitby, North Yorkshire, YO21 1RE.
Tel: 01947 602908 | www.whitbymuseum.org.uk/d12/photo/index.htm

Sutcliffe worked in Whitby from the mid-1870's until his death in 1942, and the Whitby Literary and Philosophical Society holds the copyright on many of his images, which form a major part of the library's photographic collection. (Copies of his photographs can be seen at and obtained from the Sutcliffe Gallery, 1 Flowergate, Whitby, YO21 3BA; 01947 602239; www.sutcliffe-gallery.co.uk.)

Tilley, H H
See Fowke, above.

Thomson, John
Museum of London, 150 London Wall, London, EC2Y 5HN | Tel: 020 7001 9844.
www.museumoflondon.org.uk/English/Collections/1700Today/Photographs.htm

Pictures of London street life, 1870s.

Tunny, James Good
Edinburgh Room, Edinburgh Central Library. 9 George IV Bridge, Edinburgh, EH1 1EG.
Tel: 0131 242 8030 | www.edinburgh.gov.uk/libraries

A small collection of Tunny's work dating from the 1850s and 1860s.

Valentine, James
Department of Special Collections, University of St Andrews Library, North Street, St Andrews, Fife, KY16 9TR | Tel: 01334 462339.
http://special.st-andrews.ac.uk/saspecial

Around 120,000 images (from about 1860-1930) representing the activities of a company that moved on from portrait photography to become one of the world's largest publishers of picture postcards.

Vandyk
See Bassano, above.

Vick, William
Ipswich Record Office, Gatacre Road, Ipswich, Suffolk, IP1 2LQ.
Tel: 01473 584541 | www.suffolk.gov.uk/sro

Glass plate negatives from the years 1864-1920.

Walmsley, Charles
See Ashley, above.

Watson, Tom
Whitby Museum, Pannett Park, Whitby, North Yorkshire, YO21 1RE.
Tel: 01947 602908 | www.whitbymuseum.org.uk/d12/photo/index.htm

A collection of photographs from the late Victorian and Edwardian periods.

Weiss, Paul
See Fowke, above.

Welchman, Edgar & Son
Bassetlaw Museum, Arncott House, 40 Grove Street, Retford, Nottinghamshire, DN22 6LD | Tel: 01777 713749 | www.bassetlawmuseum.org.uk/index.asp?page=welchman

The Welchman archive has over 27,000 photographs of North Nottinghamshire places and people taken in the period 1910-1960.

Went, Douglas
Essex Record Office, Wharf Road, Chelmsford, CM2 6YT | Tel: 01245 244644. www.essex.gov.uk/Libraries-Archives/Record-Office/Pages/Record-Office.aspx

Violet's memories of working for Went form part of an oral history record created by Violet and Henry Chaplin.

Whyte, David
Inverness Museum & Art Gallery, Castle Wynd, Inverness, IV2 3EB.
Tel: 01463 237114 | http://inverness.highland.museum

Around 140,000 negatives and prints make up the collection from the David Whyte studios. Whyte practised in Inverness from the 1860s until 1905, and his widow continued with the business for some years after his death. But later proprietors kept the original studio name, until the business eventually closed in 1985. Most of the images in the collection date from the studio's twentieth century activities.

Wilson, Christopher
Lowestoft Record Office, Clapham Road Lowestoft, Suffolk, NR32 1DR.
Tel: 01502 405350 | www.suffolk.gov.uk/sro

A collection of over 500 prints and 100 glass negatives, c1900-1940. (Wilson is also represented in a Lowestoft Photographers collection, for which see Bevan, above.)

Wilson, George Washington
Special Libraries and Archives, King's College, Aberdeen, AB24 3SW.
Tel: 01224 272598 | http://ibase.abdn.ac.uk

A collection of over 40,000 glass negatives from the second half of the nineteenth century.

Wood & Son
Perth Museum & Art Gallery, George street, Perth, PH7 3NF | Tel: 01738 632488.
www.pkc.gov.uk/Education+and+learning/Museums+and+galleries/Perth+Museum+and+Art+Gallery/Collections/Photographic+Collection

The Woods were printers and publishers. The collection (of over 1,000 negatives and the two albums of prints) preserves of the images of several Perthshire photographers who worked with them.

Wood, William Hugh
Orkney Library & Archive, 44 Junction Road, Kirkwall, Orkney, KW15 1AG.
Tel: 01856 873166; www.orkneylibrary.org.uk/html/photographers.htm

The Orkney Photographic Archive holds about 1,000 glass plates from the 1870s and later. (Wood, a postmaster, doesn't strictly qualify for the definition of studio photographer, but he was the nearest Orcadian equivalent for many years.)

3. Online repositories

Whilst many of the repositories already mentioned have placed a selection of their photographic holdings on their websites, there are a few archives (of varied potential value) that can be searched only online. Some are privately held and not available for physical production; others, though related to a physical repository, have a wholly independent and fully searchable virtual existence. They are dealt with here in alphabetical order of website title.

Alfred Seaman Photographic Archive
http://alfredseaman.webs.com

Images dating from the late nineteenth and early twentieth centuries are being regularly added to a site that will eventually contain many thousands of examples of Seaman's work,

Francis Frith
http://www.francisfrith.com

The site's images, dating from the 1860s onward, comprise about one-third of the 360,000 topographical photographs in the Francis Frith Collection. Subjects are fully searchable, but there is no way of identifying which of the firm's many employees took any given picture.

Harrow Photos
www.harrowphotos.com

Harrow Photos is the website for photos from the Harrow-on-the-Hill branch of Hills and Saunders, a studio chain specialising in serving academic and military centres. When the Harrow branch closed, its estimated 80,000 glass negatives were cared for by Harrow School, before passing into private ownership in 2009. Over 13,000 of these images (dating from 1866 onward) have so far been scanned and placed on the website. The holdings can be searched by title/name, description and negative number. Since Hills and Saunders was a chain with many employees, the site is excellent for exploring the work of the studio, but not helpful in identifying the work of individual photographers.

Hughes Collection
www.thehughescollection.co.uk/index.html

These images, selected and scanned from a privately held series of around 2,000 glass negatives, are the work of Joseph Hughes of Bromsgrove. Attendant detail is limited, but sitters are identified in some cases.

J Palmer Clarke / Ramsey & Muspratt Portrait Collection
http://hipweb.cambridgeshire.gov.uk/cambscoll/indexRM.html

This is a site devoted to photographs produced by a series of occupants of a studio at Post Office Terrace, Cambridge. (More details are given under 'Clarke' in the 'Single-studio collections' section of this chapter.)

The website is home to a project whereby tens of thousands of images will be copied and made available to researchers online. Completion of the site will clearly take time, and the main effort so far appears to have been put into photographs from the early twentieth century. There are ten search categories (by client's surname, date of taking, client's street, workplace, military unit and so on) but there is no facility for identifying photographers. Eventually, when the date index is fully operational, it should be possible to use it to locate pictures taken during the occupancy of a specific photographer. But that is not yet the case.

Lilian Ream Collection
www.lilianream.org.uk/about_the_collection.htm

In 1993 the Cambridgeshire County Council handed over between 150,000 and 200,000 negatives to the newly-formed Lilian Ream Exhibition Gallery Trust, which is undertaking a long-term project to make images from the collection available online. Conservation of deteriorating negatives is proving expensive and slow, but some photographs are on the website, along with some information about the photographer, the collection and relevant publications.

See also the entry for Lilian Ream in the 'Single-studio collections' section of this chapter.

4. Single items in repositories

The emphasis so far has been on collections. There are, of course, many other documents in the archives that relate to photographers, but only a researcher armed with a specific name or studio address will find them. A few illustrations will serve to indicate something of the possibilities. (Since to withhold them would seem churlish, contact details are given. But it must be emphasised that these represent no more than a scattering of random examples.)

The Bristol Record Office, for instance, holds some documents relating to William Friese Greene. In addition to a number of portraits by him, there's a photograph of his birthplace, a memorandum from him to a firm of stationers, a retrospective pamphlet and some press cuttings relating to his funeral. But these items are held separately rather than as a Friese Greene collection. (Bristol Record Office, 'B' Bond Warehouse, Smeaton Road, Bristol, BS1 6XN. Tel:0117 922 4224 | http://archives.bristol.gov.uk/dserve.)

The Kent Archives Service holds plans for several new photographic studios. In two cases (Youens and Daines) the photographer is indicated in the catalogue. Others are identified simply by address, which acts as a useful reminder that it's worth searching by premises as well as by the practitioner's name. (Kent Archives Service, County Hall, Maidstone, ME14 1XQ; 01622 694363; www.kentarchives.org.uk.)

The Leicester & Rutland Record office has invoices from John Burton for taking portraits and for providing lamps for lectures. (The Record Office for Leicestershire, Leicester & Rutland, Long Street, Wigston Magna, Leicester, LE18 2AH | Tel: 0116 257 1080. www.leics.gov.uk/record_office.)

In the Warwickshire County Record office can be found the 1853-1859 ledger of Samuel Buckle, a photographer and camera maker of Leamington Spa. (Warwickshire County Record Office, Priory Park, Cape Road, Warwick, CV34 4JS | Tel: 01926 738959. www.warwickshire.gov.uk/countyrecordoffice.)

West Glamorgan's Archive Service is home to R T Cartwright's account book for the years 1863-1867. The fact that Cartwright was a Bristol photographer shows that it can sometimes be worth searching a little farther afield than at first seems necessary. (West Glamorgan Archive Service, Civic Centre, Oystermouth Road, Swansea, SA1 3SN. Tel: 01792 636589 | www.swansea.gov.uk/index.cfm?articleid=406.)

Varied press cuttings in the Oxfordshire Record Office include reports of Messrs Baume setting up temporary premises in Star Hotel Yard in 1855, Robert Hills giving up the haircutting side of his business in 1862, and Abbott Booty being declared bankrupt in 1878. (Oxfordshire Record Office, St Luke's Church, Temple Road, Cowley, Oxford, OX4 2HT | Tel: 01865 398200 | www.oxfordshire.gov.uk/oro.)

These holdings make up a mere handful of examples, but they underline the point: it's worth checking repositories in the appropriate town or county, to see if any evidence of the ancestral photographer has been preserved. That, incidentally, can mean investigating academic institutions, museums and local studies libraries as well as record offices.

It may be possible to begin the search online. Many repositories' websites now offer access to at least some parts of their catalogue, and many other catalogues or part-catalogues can be explored via the National Register of Archives, the Scottish Archive Network, the Archon directory, Access to Archives, the Archives Hub or Cornucopia.

The National Register of Archives (NRA)
www.nationalarchives.gov.uk/nra/default.asp

The NRA, created by the National Archives, is a national finding aid for records. It can be searched by personal and family name, place name and corporate name. (Since a photographer's personal name and business name were often the same, it seems sensible to seek him in both categories.)

The Scottish Archive Network (SCAN)
www.scan.org.uk/aboutus/indexonline.htm

The SCAN online catalogue allows researchers to discover information about more than 20,000 publicly available collections of historical records in archives throughout Scotland. (Information about thousands of additional private records can be found in the catalogue of the National Register of Archives for Scotland, which can be found at www.nas.gov.uk/onlineRegister.)

Archon
www.nationalarchives.gov.uk/archon/default.htm

The Archon directory, hosted by the National Archives, allows searchers to identify repositories, checking them by region and discovering which may be of interest. Contact information is provided and links are offered to NRA information and to online finding aids.

Access to Archives (A2A)
www.nationalarchives.gov.uk/a2a/default.aspx

Yet another National Archives initiative, A2A offers an extensive menu of specific English and Welsh catalogues that can be searched, but will also run a broader regional sweep. Initial findings (brief description and location) can lead on to very detailed information about specific documents.

The Archives Hub
www.archiveshub.ac.uk

Based at the University of Manchester, the Archives Hub represents over 180 academic institutions, serving as finding aid for material in their collections.

Cornucopia
www.cornucopia.org.uk/html

This site, maintained by the Museums, Libraries and Archives Council, has information about more than 6,000 collections in the UK's museums. It offers quick search, advanced search and browsing facilities.

It isn't wise, however, to assume that all the necessary checking can be done online. The task of digitising catalogues is huge, and much work remains to be done. It may be, therefore, that the vital discovery can be reached only via an onsite card index or finding aid. There is still much about which the Internet is silent.

CHAPTER FIVE
Career and biographical information in print

Individual high-street photographers have received rather less attention in print than have well-bred amateurs and art photographers. This is inevitable. The pioneering work of so many early amateurs gives them historical importance, while the originality of the artist demands to be noticed. A few high-street photographers - people like Henry Peach Robinson and Frank Meadow Sutcliffe - did succeed in straddling two worlds: they managed both to run a business and to earn a reputation for creativity. Most studio professionals, however, did a workmanlike job, taking a pride in their products, providing a valued service to their local community, and doing nothing to attract a biographer's attention. Nevertheless, there are some books and articles that focus on individual professionals and their studios.

1. Single-studio works

The list that follows (mainly books, but occasionally articles) is made up of works devoted to a specific studio or photographer. There are, however, one or two exceptions: general works that devote a whole section to a single photographer have been mentioned, as have works that focus on just two early photographers or studios. Anything more diverse in its treatment of named photographers will be found in the next section of this chapter.

It should also be noted that some works are devoted to individual photographers without giving very much information about their lives or careers. Sometimes a brief introduction is simply an appetiser for a main course consisting of examples of the photographer's work. (In such cases, incidentally, the studio-bound aspects of that work are often poorly represented.)

The list is presented in alphabetical order of photographers rather than authors.

Abery, P B
Welson, John (ed.), *Photographs of Radnorshire: P B Abery* (Little Logaston: Logaston Press, 2008).

Annan, J Craig
Buchanan, William, *Art of the photographer: J Craig Annan* (Edinburgh: National Galleries of Scotland, 1992).

Bagshaw, Luke
Tuffrey, Peter & Day, James, *Luke Bagshaw's photographs of old Doncaster* (Rossington: Bond Publications, 1984).
Tuffrey, Peter, *Doncaster: through the lens of Luke Bagshaw* (Stroud: History Press, 2008).

Bassano, Alexander
Hillier, Bevis, *Victorian Studio Photographs* (London: Ash & Grant, 1975).

Beard, Richard
Heathcote, Pauline & Bernard, *Richard Beard, an ingenious and enterprising patentee* in *History of Photography*, volume 3, number 4 (London: Taylor & Francis, October 1979).

Begbie, Thomas
Patterson, David & Rock, Joe, *Thomas Begbie's Edinburgh - a mid-Victorian portrait* (Edinburgh: John Donald, 1992).

Bourne, Samuel
Sampson, G, *The success of Samuel Bourne in India*, in *History of Photography*, volume 16, number 4 (London: Taylor & Francis, 1992).

Brookes, Warwick
Linkman, Audrey, *Warwick Brookes, Warwick Brookes and Warwick Brookes*, in *The PhotoHistorian*, 82 (London: Royal Photographic Society, autumn 1988).

Broom, Christina
Atkinson, Diane, *Mrs Broom's suffragette photographs (The Photo-Library 10)* (London: Dirk Nishen, 1989).

Brown, Theodore
Herbert, Stephen, *Theodore Brown's magic pictures: the art and inventions of a multi-media pioneer* (London: Production Box, 1997).

Carrick, William
Ashbee, Felicity & Lawson, Julie, *William Carrick 1827-1878* (Edinburgh: National Galleries of Scotland, 1987).

Clarke, John Palmer
Statham, Margaret & Serjeant, William, *Victorian Bury St Edmunds in photographs* (Ipswich: Suffolk County Archives/County Libraries, 1980).

Claudet, Antoine
Sevey, Linda Vance, *The question of style in daguerreotype and calotype portraits by Antoine Claudet* (Henrietta, New York: Rochester Institute of Technology, 1977).
Pickering, B M, *A Claudet FRS: a memoir* (London: B M Pickering, 1868).

Coburn, Alvin Langdon
Gernsheim, Helmut & Alison, *Alvin Langdon Coburn: photographer* (New York: Praeger, 1966).

Cundall, William
McLean, R, *Joseph Cundall, a Victorian publisher: notes on his life and a checklist of his books* (Pinner, Private Libraries Association, 1976).

Edis, Olive
Childs, Alan, Sampson, Ashley & Nunn, Cyril, *Face to Face, Sheringham, Norfolk: the remarkable story of Olive Edis and Cyril Nunn* (Tiverton: Halsgrove, 2005).
Neale, Shirley, *Olive Edis (1876-1955)* in *History of photography*, volume 16, number 4 (London: Taylor & Francis, winter 1992).

Edwards, B J
Welsford, S F W, *B J Edwards, Victorian photographer, inventor and entrepreneur* in *History of photography* volume 13, number 2 (London: Taylor & Francis, June 1989).

Elliott & Fry
Hillier, Bevis, *Victorian Studio Photographs* (London: Ash & Grant, 1975).

Frith, Francis
Hudson, Roger (ed.), *Travels of a Victorian photographer: the photographs of Francis Frith* (London: Folio Society, 2001).
Jay, Bill, *Victorian cameraman: Francis Frith's views of rural England* (Newton Abbot, 1973).
Talbot, Joanna & Eakins, Rosemary, *Francis Frith (Masters of Photography series)* (London: Macdonald, 1985).
There are, in addition, numerous picture books based on Frith's photographs and organised around locations (e.g. *Photographic memories of Yorkshire* and *Grandpa's Essex as seen by Victorian photographer Francis Frith*) or themes (e.g. *Canals and inland waterways* and *Francis Frith's Scottish castles*).

Gibson, John Pattison
Ham, Philip, *Portraits of Northumberland: the postcards of Gibson and son* (Hexham: Ergo Press, 2006).
Jedrzejezyk, Isabella, Gard, R N & Bradley AG, *John Pattison Gibson 1838-1912, Northumbrian photographer* (Newcastle: Side Galleries, 1982).

Hayes, William
Buchanan, Terry, *William Hayes, 1871-1940: York photographic artist* (Beverley: Hutton, 1986).

Hoppé, Emil Otto
Beresford, J D, *Taken from life* (London: Collins, 1922).
Hoppé, E O, *Hundred thousand exposures: the success of a photographer* (London: Focal Press, 1945).
Pepper, T (ed), *Camera Portraits by E O Hoppé, 1878-1972* (London: National Portrait Gallery, 1978).

Howe, H L
Cuppleditch, David, *H L Howe, a twentieth century Louth photographer, 1897-1959* (London: Dilke, 1988).

Hughes, Joseph
O'Brien, Terry, *Bromsgrove's Victorian photographic treasury: the Hughes collection* (Stroud: History Press, 2008).

Jackson, Magnus
Payne, Susan, *Magnus Jackson and the black art* in *Journal of the Perthshire Society of Natural Science*, volume 17 (Perth: Perthshire Society of Natural Science, 2003). This article can also be located online at www.perthshirebigtreecountry.co.uk/magnusjackson/documents/Magnus%20Jackson%20and%20the%20Black%20Art.pdf

Keene, Richard
Craven, Maxwell (ed.), *Keene's Derby* (Derby, Breedon Books, 1993).

Lewis, Thomas
Whybrow, John, *How does your Birmingham grow? From the John Whybrow collection of old and new photographs* (Birmingham: John Whybrow, 1972).

Longstaff, Alice
Shannon, Izzy & Woolrych, Frank, *Alice's album; the story of a Hebden Bridge photographer's studio* (Hebden Bridge: Milltown Memories, 2004).

Martin, Paul
Flukinger, Roy, Schaaf, Larry & Meacham, Standish, *Paul Martin: Victorian photographer* (London: Gordon Fraser, 1978).
Haworth-Booth, Mark, *A Yarmouth holiday (The Photo-Library 4)* (London: Dirk Nishen, 1988).
Jay, Bill, *Victorian candid camera: Paul Martin 1864-1944* (Newton Abbot: David & Charles, 1973).
Martin, Paul, *Victorian snapshots* (London: Country Life, 1939).

Moffat, John
Moffat John S, *John Moffat, pioneer Scottish photographic artist, 1819-1894* (Eastbourne: JSM Publishing, 1990) [SoG shelf mark: FH/MOF].
Moffat, John S, *John Moffat of Edinburgh: a Victorian photographer in the family* in *Genealogists' Magazine*, volume 24, number 6 (London, Society of Genealogists, June 1993).

Muybridge, Eadweard
Hendricks, Gordon, *Eadweard Muybridge: the father of the motion picture* (Mineola, New York: Dover, 2001).

Nicholls, Horace W
Buckland, Gail, *Golden summer: Edwardian photographs of Horace W Nicholls* (London: Pavilion Books, 1989).

Nunn, Cyril
Childs, Alan, Sampson, Ashley & Nunn, Cyril, *Face to Face, Sheringham, Norfolk: the remarkable story of Olive Edis and Cyril Nunn* (Tiverton: Halsgrove, 2005).

Ream, Lilian
Fosbrook-Ream, Violet, *Lilian Ream: a life in photography* (Cambridge: Cambridge County Council, Libraries and Information Service, 1992).
Ream, Lilian & Golding, Eric, *Reams of Wisbech: scenes from a fenland studio* (Cambridge: Cambridgeshire Libraries and Information Service, 1987).
Wilkinson, Colin & Bell, Robert, *From cradle to grave in a fenland town* (Liverpool: Bluecoat Press, 2010).

Rejlander, Oscar
Fielding, A G, *Rejlander in Wolverhampton: his sponsorship by William Parke*, in *History of Photography*, volume 11, number 1 (London: Taylor & Francis, Jan-March 1987).
Jones, Edgar Yoxall, *Father of art photography: O G Rejlander 1813-1875* (Newton Abbott: David & Charles, 1973).

Righton, John William
Norgate, Thomas Linney, *From pedagogy to photography: the life and work of John William Righton* (Petersfield: 613 Books, 2008).

Robinson, Henry Peach
Coleman, David, *Henry Peach Robinson: Victorian photographer* (Austin: University of Texas, 20010).
Harker, Margaret F, *Henry Peach Robinson, master of photographic art, 1830-1901* (Oxford: Basil Blackwell, 1988).

Sarony, Oliver
Bayliss, Ann & Paul, *Photographers in mid-nineteenth century Scarborough: the Sarony Years: a history and dictionary* (Scarborough, A M Bayliss, 1998) [SoG shelf mark: Shelf 9 (YR/LOC)].

Scrivens, Leonard
Tuffrey, Peter, *Doncaster, from the Scrivens collection* (Doncaster: Nonsuch, 1995).

Shaw, John William & Alfred
Duckworth, Alan & Halsall, Jim, *By rivers, through valleys and dales: a journey through Lancashire and Yorkshire with Edwardian photographers John William and Alfred Shaw* (Blackpool: Landy, 2009).

Silvy, Camille
Frecker, Paul, *Camille Silvy and the English press* in History of Photography, volume 33, number 4 (London: Taylor & Francis, autumn 2009).
Haworth-Booth, Mark, *Camille Silvy: river scene, France* (Malibu, California: J Paul Getty Museum, 1992).
Haworth-Booth, Mark, *Camille Silvy: photographer of modern life 1834-1910* (London: National Portrait Gallery, 2010).

Spalding, Fred
Jarvis, Stan, *The world of Fred Spalding: photographs of Essex 1860-1949* (Chelmsford: Essex Record Office, 1992) [SoG shelf mark: ES/PER].

Spanton, William
Statham, Margaret & Serjeant, William, *Victorian Bury St Edmunds in photographs* (Ipswich: Suffolk County Archives/County Libraries, 1980).

Speight, Edward Hall & family
Frearson, John, *Edward Hall Speight and his family - Rugby's photographers* (Rugby: John Frearson Publications, 2009).
Frearson, John, *The Speights of Rugby - photographers* (Rugby: John Frearson Publications, 2009).

Sturdee, Thankfull
Sturdee, Thankfull, *Reminiscences of old Deptford: reproduced from old prints, drawings etc., photographed by Thankfull Sturdee* (London: Henry Richardson, 1895).
Sturdee, Thankfull, *One man's Deptford: a selection from the photographs of Thankfull Sturdee* (London: London Borough of Lewisham, 1980).

Sutcliffe, Frank Meadow
Hiley, Michael, *Frank Sutcliffe, photographer of Whitby* (London: Gordon Fraser, 1974).
Shaw, Bill Eglon, *Frank Meadow Sutcliffe, photographer: a selection of his work* (Whitby: Sutcliffe Gallery, 1974, revised 1982).
Shaw, Bill Eglon, *Frank Meadow Sutcliffe: a second selection* (Whitby: Sutcliffe Gallery, 1978).
Shaw, Michael, *Frank Meadow Sutcliffe, photographer: a third selection* (Whitby: Sutcliffe Gallery, 1990).
Shaw, Michael, *Frank Meadow Sutcliffe: a fourth selection* (Whitby: Sutcliffe Gallery, 1998).

All the Sutcliffe Gallery books have a brief introduction to a selection of photographs. The third in the series has the most information, but the fourth also includes a brief biography.

Taunt, Henry
Brown, Bryan (ed.), *The England of Henry Taunt Victorian photographer* (London: Routledge & Kegan Paul, 1973).
Graham, Malcolm, *Henry Taunt of Oxford: a Victorian photographer* (Oxford: Oxford Illustrated Press, 1973).

Thomas, John
Woollen, Hilary & Crawford, Alistair, *John Thomas, 1838-1905: photographer* (Llandysul: Gorner Press, 1977).

Thomson, John
Ovenden, Richard, *John Thomson (1837-1921): photographer* (Edinburgh: Stationery Office, 1997).
Thomson, J & Smith, Adolphe, *Victorian London street life in historic photographs* (New York: Dover, 1994).
White, Steven, *John Thomson: life and photographs* (London: Thanes & Hudson, 1985).

Titshall, Leonard and Ralph
Kindred, David & Smith, Roger, *In a long day: the Titshall photographs of farm and village life* (Ipswich: Long Pond Publishing, 1999).
Kindred, David & Smith, Roger, *Just a moment: Titshall photographs of working lives* (Ipswich: Long Pond Publishing, 2007).
The Titshall brothers really started in business a few years too late to feature legitimately in this list. Since books focusing on the work of itinerant professionals are so unusual, I have turned a blind eye to my own transgression.

Tunny, James G
Bukits, Julian, *A study of James G Tunny, 1820-1887: photographer and political radical, Edinburgh* (Edinburgh: Julian Bukits, 2009).

Valentine, James
Kemp, Martin (ed.), *Mood of the moment: masterworks of photography from the University of St Andrews* (St Andrews: University of St Andrews, 1995).
Smart, R N, *Famous throughout the world: Valentine & Sons Ltd, Dundee*, in *Review of Scottish Culture*, 4 (Edinburgh: John Donald, 1988).

***Whitlock*, Henry**
Whybrow, John, *How does your Birmingham grow? From the John Whybrow collection of old and new photographs* (Birmingham: John Whybrow, 1972).

***Willey*, Joseph**
Cuppleditch, David, *Joseph Willey: a Victorian Lincolnshire photographer, 1829-1893* (Cheddar: Charles Skilton, 1987).

***Wilson*, Christopher**
Robb, Ian G, *Images of Lowestoft: the photographs of Christopher Wilson* (Stroud: Sutton Publishing, 2002).

***Wilson*, George Washington**
Durie, Alistair & Mellor, Roy, *George Washington Wilson and the Scottish railways* (Keighley: Kennedy Brothers, in association with the University of Aberdeen, 1983).
Peterich, Gerda, '*G.W.W.*' in *Image*, volume 5, number 10 (Rochester, New York: International Museum of Photography, December 1956).
Taylor, Roger, *George Washington Wilson - Artist and photographer (1823-93)* (Aberdeen: Aberdeen University Press, 1981).

***Yerbury* family**
Cant, Malcolm & Yerbury, Trevor, *Yerbury: a photographic collection, 1850-1993* (Edinburgh: Mercat Press, 1993).

2. Multi-studio works

Works that deal with a number of early photographers tend to focus on the most eminent, paying generous attention to innovators and pioneers - many of whom were amateurs - and to those whose work is seen as having particular artistic value. Where studio photographers are included, they are often the best known - either because their work beyond the studio walls attracted attention, or because they catered for the upper end of the market and, in some cases, earned a reputation for their portraits of the rich and famous. There are, however, some exceptions to this generalisation: the more tightly focused a multi-studio work is, either geographically or in specialist theme, the less predictably restricted its choice of photographers is likely to be.

The convention of listing alphabetically by author has been reverted to in this section. Additional (usually brief) notes seek to give readers some indication of what to expect.

Adamson, Keith I P, *Early provincial studios*, in *The Photographic Journal*, volume 127, number 2 (London: Royal Photographic Society, February 1987) [A].

Adamson, Keith I P, *More early studios*, in *The Photographic Journal*, volume 128, number 1 (London: Royal Photographic Society, January 1988) [B].

Adamson, Keith I P, *More early studios (Part 2)*, in *The Photographic Journal*, volume 128, number 7 (London: Royal Photographic Society, July 1988) [C].

This series of articles studies the first daguerreotype photographers in 28 towns or counties. It may help researchers to know which articles cover which locations:

Cambridgeshire	Cambridge	C
Cheshire	Chester	C
Devon	Exeter	B
	Plymouth	A
Durham	Sunderland	C
Essex	(whole county)	C
Gloucestershire	Bristol	A
	Cheltenham	A
Hampshire	Southampton	B
Lancashire	Liverpool	A
	Manchester	A
Leicestershire	Leicester	C
Lincolnshire	(whole county)	C
Middlesex	London	C
Norfolk	Norwich	C
Nottinghamshire	Nottingham	A
Oxfordshire	Oxford	B
Somerset	Bath	A
Sussex	Brighton	A
Warwickshire	Birmingham	B
Worcestershire	Worcester	C
Yorkshire	(parts of county)	B
	Harrogate	C
	Hull	C
	Leeds	B
	Scarborough	B
	Sheffield	B
	York	C

Baden, Pritchard H, *The Photographic studios of Europe* (London: Piper & Carter, 1882; print-to-order edition - LaVergne: Kessinger Publishing, 2010).

This book reports visits to a wide range of studios, most of them in Britain. Photographic printing, astronomical photography and even prison studios are covered, but most visits were to more conventional studio photographers. There are snatches of interviews with principals, and senior employees of the larger establishments are sometimes mentioned. The wealth of detail ranges from collodion recipes and negative storage systems to working hours, fees and the management of light (including the avoidance of reflections from bald heads). Since this could prove such a valuable source for researchers whose target photographers are included, a list of the British commercial studios seems appropriate:

Annan, T & R	Autotype Works (Sawyer & Bird)
Barton, W Harvey	Bassano, Alexander
Bedford, Francis	Blanchard, Valentine
Brown, Barnes & Bell	Downey, W & D
Elliott & Fry	England, William
Faulkner, Robert	Fergus, John
Hills & Saunders	Hughes, Jabez
Jennings, Payne	Lafosse, Augustus
Laws, P Maitland	Mayall & Co (Brighton)
Mayland, William	Midwinter, W H
Platinotype Company	Robinson, Henry Peach
Russell & Sons	Sarony, Oliver
Slingsby, Robert	Taylor, A & G
Valentine, James	Van der Weyde
Wane, Marshall	Window & Grove
Woodbury, Walter	

Beaton, Cecil & ***Buckland***, Gail, *The magic image, the genius of photography from 1839 to the present day* (London: Weidenfeld & Nicolson, 1975).

Around 200 photographers are mentioned, but only the better-known studio professionals are included.

Browne, Turner & ***Partnow***, Elaine, *Macmillan biographical encyclopaedia of photographic artists and innovators* (London & New York: Macmillan, 1983).

There are entries for around 2,000 individuals. Most of them, inevitably, fall outside the definition of studio photographer.

Buchanan, William, *Photography comes to Glasgow: a survey of fifteen years 1839-1854* in *Scottish Photography Bulletin* (Edinburgh: Scottish Society for the History of Photography, Spring 1988).

The title of this tightly focused article is self-explanatory.

Budge, Adrian, *Early photography in Leeds 1839-1870* (Leeds: Leeds Art Galleries, 1981).

Though largely given over to illustrations, this includes a historical essay and an index of Leeds photographers (which accounts for it also being listed in the chapter on photographer directories).

Budge, Adrian, *Yorkshire and photography - the early years*, in *The Photographic Collector*, volume 4, number 1 (London: Bishopsgate Press, spring 1983).

The main emphasis is on amateur photography, but there is some treatment of the county's early studios.

Cox, James Stevens, *Ilchester and district occasional papers No. 82: Itinerant traders, craftsmen and street entertainers - also photographers who visited Ilchester in the 19th and early 20th century* (St Sampson, Guernsey: Toucan Press, 1988).

The title is self-explanatory.

Dimond, Frances & **Taylor**, Roger, *Crown and camera: the royal family and photography, 1842-1910* (Harmondsworth: Penguin, 1987).

Brief notes on nearly 100 royal photographers (many of them studio professionals) are included. There is also a chronology of photographers granted royal warrants during the reign of Queen Victoria.

Fletcher, Simon, *Cheltenham's first photographers*, in *Cheltenham Local History Society Journal*, 3 (Cheltenham: Cheltenham Local History Society, 1985).

The article deals with the period 1841-1856. Copies are held at the Gloucestershire Archives and the Cheltenham Local Studies centre.

Hannavy, John, *Masters of Victorian photography* (New York: Holmes & Meier, 1976).

Studio photographers make up a fairly small proportion of the handful of chapters that are devoted to individuals. The index identifies a few more professionals who are mentioned in passing.

Hannavy, John (ed.), *Encyclopedia of nineteenth century photography* (Abingdon: Routledge, 2005).

Many studio photographers are included in this 1,736-page volume, and the entries are generally much fuller than those found in other multi-studio sources. But it's a book intended for libraries, few of which will be able to countenance its £300+ price tag. It can be found at the British Library, and a full list of entries, at www.gbhap-us.com/ncphotog/entries.html, will help researchers decide whether they need to consult it.

Harker, Margaret, *The Linked Ring: the secession in photography in Britain, 1882-1910* (London: Royal Photographic Society & Heinemann, 1979).

The concerns of the Linked Ring were primarily artistic, but the group's members included a handful of eminent studio photographers.

Haworth-Booth, Mark (ed.), *The golden age of British photography 1839-1900* (Millerton, New York: Aperture, 1984).

A series of essays is followed by biographies and career details of around 40 photographers. Some of these are studio professionals, but they tend to be the best known.

Heathcote, Bernard & Pauline, *The feminine influence: aspects of the role of women in the evolution of photography in the British Isles*, in *History of Photography*, volume 12, number 3 (Abingdon: Taylor & Francis, 1988).

This presents, in table form, some details of 22 women who ran professional studios.

Heathcote, Bernard & Pauline, *A faithful likeness: the first photographic portrait studios in the British Isles, 1841 to 1855* (Lowdham: Bernard & Pauline Heathcote, 2002).

The Heathcotes' invaluable account of early studios includes biographical notes (of varying length) on studio professionals operating during the given period. There is also a directory of photographers organised by location.

Heathcote, P F, *The first ten years of the daguerreotype in Nottingham*, in *History of Photography*, volume 2, number 4 (Abingdon: Taylor & Francis, October 1978).

A study of Nottingham's earliest practitioners.

Isaacs, J V, *Devon photograph index* in *Devon Family Historian*, number 46 (Plympton: Devonshire FHS, April 1988) [SoG shelf mark: DE/PER].

This continues the theme of the article by Sheila and Tom Jewell (below).

Kelly, Stephen F, *Victorian Lakeland photographers* (Shrewsbury: Swan Hill Press, 1991).

A number of the area's professionals are included among the book's ten photographer profiles. [SoG shelf mark: PR/PHO].

Jewell, Sheila & Tom, *Family photographs* in *Devon Family Historian*, number 45 (Plympton: Devonshire FHS, January 1988) [SoG shelf mark: DE/PER].

Whilst making no claim to be a directory of studios, the article seeks to date the work of some Devon photographers from order serial numbers.

Lenman, Robin (ed.), *The Oxford companion to the photograph* (Oxford: Oxford University Press, 2005).

This valuable reference source for all manner of photographic topics includes brief biographies of a number of the better-known studio photographers. There is some useful coverage of British photographers who set up studios overseas.

Lewis, Mark, *Tenby in camera: a history of photography and Tenby photographers* (Tenby: Tenby Museum & Art Gallery, 1999).

A 16-page booklet, written to accompany an exhibition of Tenby photography. It seems difficult to locate.

Mathews, Oliver, *Early photographs and early photographers: a survey in dictionary form* (London: Reedminster Publications, 1973).
Entries include a good selection of studio photographers, but the information about them is often very limited. This was an early attempt to document a range of photographers and should probably be thought of as superseded.

Pepper, Terence, *High society photographs, 1897-1914* (London: National Portrait Gallery, 1998).

Published to accompany an exhibition, this book looks at the photographing of (essentially) Edwardian society and appends brief biographies of over 20 photographers. Coverage is not confined to the most famous studios.

Scott, C, *The life and times of Castle Terrace: a daguerreotype studio in Exeter* in *History of Photography*, volume 15, number 1 (London: Taylor & Francis, spring 1991).

William Gill and John Jury ran studios at Castle Terrace.

Stevenson, Sara, *Masterpieces of photography from the Riddell Collection* (Edinburgh: National Galleries of Scotland, 1986).

Written to accompany an exhibition, this work includes biographical notes on the photographers who were represented (and who were by no means all Scottish). Lesser-known practitioners as well as major figures are included.

Turley, Raymond V, *Isle of Wight photographers, 1840-1940* (Southampton: Southampton University Libraries, 2001).

Brief biographies of around 40 photographers form part of a work that also covers newspaper articles and exhibitions. There is a strong emphasis on source materials.

Walker, Brian Mercer, *Shadows on glass* (Belfast: Appletree Press, 1976).

A collection representing the work of 13 early Ulster photographers, some of whom were amateurs and some professionals.

Williams, Shirley, *Aberystwyth photographers of yesteryear* in *Cardiganshire FHS Journal*, volume 2, number 5 (Ceredigion: Cardiganshire FHS, June 2000) [SoG shelf mark: WS/PER].

The title is self-explanatory.

Researchers are reminded that a number of the printed directories of photographers, listed in an earlier chapter, also contain some biographical and career information.

It should also be noted that more broadly based works on early photography often contain useful snippets of information about studio professionals, so the index of such a volume is always worth checking. This is especially true of works dealing specifically with early studio photography, several of which are listed in the general bibliography at the end of this book.

CHAPTER SIX
Career and biographical information online

Much of the information available online will be found on the websites mentioned in 'Material in Archives'. But there are other sources scattered across the ether. Such sources are often the products of enthusiasts, and enthusiasm is no guarantee of scholarship. So their reliability is something for the individual researcher to judge. At best, they offer the results of serious and conscientious research. At worst, they suggest possibilities for further, and perhaps more critical, investigation. It would seem inappropriate, at any rate, to deprive researchers of the opportunity to exercise their own judgement.

1. Single-studio sources

The list that follows covers websites or web pages devoted to the work of one (or, occasionally, two) relevant photographers, photographic families or studios. Other examples doubtless exist and await discovery.

***Annan*,** James Craig
www.photogravure.com/history/keyfigures_annan.html

***Annan*,** Thomas
http://special.lib.gla.ac.uk/exhibns/month/mar2006.html

Ault, Frederick
http://viewfinder.english-heritage.org.uk/story/intro.aspx?storyUid=20

Bedford, Francis
www.ampltd.co.uk/collections_az/Photos-1/editorial-introduction.aspx

Bird, Graystone
1. www.youtube.com/user/KEASBURYGORDON,
2. www.youtube.com/watch?v=FNFNSbo9SyQ

Blair, John Pryce
www.lizweb.net/17576.html

Bourne, Samuel
1. http://arts.jrank.org/pages/10178/Samuel-Bourne.html
2. www.harappa.com/photographers/bournesamuel.html

Bowness, Moses
http://susanpremru.webplus.net

Chadwick, W I
www.mosi.org.uk/media/33871461/w.ichadwick.pdf

Chapman, J T
www.mosi.org.uk/media/34162624/j.tchapmanltd.pdf

Clapperton, Robert
www.scottishbordercamera.com/section132697.html

Clarke, Bennett
www.localhistory.scit.wlv.ac.uk/articles/photos/photos03a.htm

Claudet, Antoine
http://19.bbk.ac.uk/index.php/19/article/viewFile/485/345

Coburn, Alvin Langdon
www.photogravure.com/history/keyfigures_coburn.html

Coe, Albert Edward
www.barrettandcoe.co.uk/barrett-and-coe-history.html

Delamotte, Phillip
http://viewfinder.english-heritage.org.uk/story/intro.aspx?storyUid=79

Downey, William
1. www.newcastle-arts-centre.co.uk/05%20william_downey__photograph.htm
2. www.newcastle-arts-centre.co.uk/downeys_photography.htm

Downey, W & D
www.rogerco.pwp.blueyonder.co.uk/pixs/downey.htm

Drummond, John
http://homepages.tesco.net/~roger.vaughan/visitors/drummond.htm

Frith, Francis
www.francisfrith.com/pageloader.asp?page=/help/frith/frithbiog.asp

Harries, D C
www.llandeilo.org/dcharries.php

Harrison, William Marsden
http://homepages.tesco.net/~roger.vaughan/visitors/sent4.htm

Henderson, Alexander L
www.vicpix.net/history.html

Hollyer, Frederick
www.vam.ac.uk/collections/photography/features/photo_focus/hollyer/index.html

Hoppé, E O
www.eohoppe.com/index.html

Howlett, Robert
1. www.suite101.com/content/robert-howlett-victorian-photographer-a189565,
2. www.photohistories.com/Photo-Histories/51/robert-howlett-and-the-power-of-photography?pg=all

Jackson, Magnus
www.perthshirebigtreecountry.co.uk/magnusjackson/index.asp

Jennings, John Payne
www.ashtead.org/people/jpj.htm

Lauder, James Stack (also known as James **Lafayette**)
1. www.vam.ac.uk/vastatic/microsites/1158_lafayette/background.php
2. www.lafayettephotography.com/Main.aspx?Id=1

Lock, Samuel
http://ocotilloroad.com/geneal/whitfield1.html

London Stereoscopic Company
www.londonstereo.com/introduction.html

Lösel, Franz Heinrich
http://homepages.tesco.net/~patio/new/losel.htm

Mayall, John Jabez Edwin
www.spartacus.schoolnet.co.uk/DSmayall.htm

Mitchell, William & William McLean
www.scottishbordercamera.com/section132697_145014.html

Monte family
http://members.shaw.ca/pauline777/Studios.html

Mudd, James T
www.mosi.org.uk/media/33871134/jamesmudd.pdf

Newton, Sydney
http://viewfinder.english-heritage.org.uk/story/intro.aspx?storyUid=82

Prout, Victor Albert
www.daao.org.au/main/read/5219

Ream, Lilian
www.wisbech-town.co.uk/lilian.htm

Reeves, Alfred
www.microscopy-uk.org.uk/mag/artdec08/bs-slides3.html

Reeves. Edward
www.edwardreeves.com/history.html

Rejlander, Oscar
www.localhistory.scit.wlv.ac.uk/articles/photos/Rejlander/Rejlander.htm

Scorer, William
www.sopse.org.uk/ixbin/hixclient.exe?a=query&p=hants&f=generic_theme%2eht
m&_IXFIRST_=1&_IXMAXHITS_=1&%3dtheme_record_id=hs%2dhs%2dscor
er_content1

Seaman, Alfred
1. http://jb3d.webs.com/alfredseaman.htm
2. http://jb3d.webs.com/stereoscopicphotography.htm

Speight, Edward Hall & family
http://johnphfrearson.host22.com/Speight-Photographers.html

Stabler, Paul
www.users.waitrose.com/~victorianphoto/stabler/stabler.htm

Stortz, Philip Christian
www.rogerco.freeserve.co.uk/stortz/stortz.htm

Sutcliffe, Frank Meadow
1. www.sutcliffe-gallery.co.uk/index.html
2. www.whitby-yorkshire.co.uk/sutcliffe/sutcliffe.htm

Taunt, Henry
1. www.henrytaunt-footsteps.co.uk/henry-taunt.htm
2. http://viewfinder.english-heritage.org.uk/story/select.aspx

Taylor, A & G
http://homepages.tesco.net/~roger.vaughan/visitors/taylor-ag.htm

Thomas, John
1. www.llgc.org.uk/index.php?id=johnthomas
2. www.rhiw.com/hanes_02/john_thomas/john_thomas_e.htm

Thomson, John
1. http://academic.reed.edu/formosa/texts/thomsonbio.html
2. www.nls.uk/thomson/index.html

Tunny, James G
www.jamesgtunny.com

Welsh, Robert John
www.irelandseye.com/aarticles/history/people/photography/country.shtm

Whitfield, George
http://ocotilloroad.com/geneal/whitfield1.html

Whitlock, Henry J
www.cartes.freeuk.com/visitors/whit.htm

Williams, T R
www.londonstereo.com/trwilliams/biography.html

Wright, Alfred and Hannah
www.nlcaonline.org.uk/page_id__508_path__0p111p.aspx

York & son
http://viewfinder.english-heritage.org.uk/story/intro.aspx?storyUid=78

2. Multi-studio sources

Some sites included in this list have a precise geographical focus. Others have a wider perspective and tend, as a result, to concentrate on the better-known names. There are also some sites where the concern is not primarily photographic, but where there is a useful overlapping of interests.

There is, of course, no way to be sure that everything relevant has been found. Even if it had been, the situation would have altered between the compilation and the publication of this list. New locations are appearing constantly, and existing locations are being expanded. A few of the sites in the following list may change little. One or two are already gathering virtual dust (though that doesn't necessarily invalidate their content). Others, however, are updated at more or less regular intervals and are worth revisiting from time to time.

Researchers are also reminded of the biographical and career details that form an adjunct to a number of online directories. A few are so full of information that they are mentioned again in this list; but the others should not be ignored.

Albumen photographs: history, science and preservation
http://albumen.conservation-us.org/library

This site allows the researcher to discover Victorian photographers using their own words. The library contains primary source material for the study of albumen photography, including many items from early photographic journals. Articles by distinguished practitioners (such as Jabez Hughes, Francis Frith, Oscar Rejlander and Henry Peach Robinson) readily catch the eye, but many of the less familiar writers were also studio professionals.

Alfred Seaman and the PCUK
http://jb3d.webs.com

The site documents the meetings of the Photographic Convention of the United Kingdom from 1886, when it was formed, until 1910. The accounts of the annual meetings vary in length, but they include a good number of references to individual members. (The pages devoted to Seaman are listed separately above.)

Archives Hub
http://archiveshub.ac.uk/search/search.html

The value of the Archives Hub for locating collections is referred to in the 'Material in archives' chapter. It is worth adding here, however, that search results offer the option of summary pages, and that these occasionally contain some quite detailed biographical information.

Artcyclopedia
www.artcyclopedia.com/media/Photographer.html

This page of the Artcyclopedia site provides links to sources for a number of well-known photographers (some of them studio professionals).

Ask Jeeves Encyclopaedia
http://uk.ask.com/wiki/Category:19th-century_photographers?qsrc=3044

Biographies of a range of early photographers appear in this online encyclopaedia, but the overwhelming majority of them seem to derive from Wikipedia (q.v.).

Bill Jay on photography
www.billjayonphotography.com

The late Bill Jay was both photographer and photographic historian, and the many and varied essays and articles on his website will repay investigation. There are pieces devoted to specific photographers – Francis Bedford, Valentine Blanchard, Nelson King Cherrill, E O Hoppé, Francis Wenham, Walter Woodbury – and discussions on subjects as varied as photographers' prices, the difficulties of photographing children and the effect of wind direction on exposure times. Some articles include passing reference to professionals who have rarely attracted attention elsewhere.

Brett Payne's Victorian & Edwardian portrait photo collection
http://freepages.genealogy.rootsweb.ancestry.com/~brett/photo2/artists.html

This page is an index to profiles of over 30 photographers in several counties. Devon is particularly well represented, with Gloucestershire coming a somewhat distant second. Elsewhere on the site (and listed in the 'Directories of early photographers' chapter) is a directory, with profiles, of Derbyshire photographers.

British picture framemakers, 1630-1950
www.npg.org.uk/research/conservation/directory-of-british-framemakers.php

Hidden away in a corner of the National Portrait Gallery's site, this directory could come up with the occasional pleasant surprise. Some photographers also made frames and therefore qualify to appear on the site. In practice, I suspect very few photographers are here, but I have (for example) found William Boswell of Norwich, whose images are not represented in the gallery's holdings, but whose career as frame maker is examined in some detail.

Cabinet card gallery
http://cabinetcardgallery.wordpress.com

An online collection and blog with some incidental (and often brief) notes on over fifty photographers whose work is represented.

Camborne Old Cornwall Society
http://camborne.wikidot.com/photographers

An article giving brief career and biographical information for around a dozen photographers in the Camborne area.

ClassyArts photographers database
www.classyarts.com/search.htm

Site-users are invited to pay for information about the required photographer. Though US-based, the site lists a good number of UK photographers. (Much of the information should, however, be available on British sites.)

There is also an index of links to biographies, some of which relate to studio photographers. These biographies are free, but they turn out, for the most part, to be Wikipedia articles.

Edinphoto
www.edinphoto.org.uk/2/2__professional_photographers.htm

In addition to housing a conventional directory of studios, this remarkable site is full of information about photography in Edinburgh and includes profiles of many practitioners. Some kind of photographic association with Edinburgh is the criterion for inclusion, but associations can be as slight as, say, contributions by outsiders to exhibitions in the city. So some unexpected names are featured.

Genealogy in Hertfordshire: postcards and other pictures
www.hertfordshire-genealogy.co.uk/data/postcards/!-postcards-frame.htm

As well as providing information on a number of the county's photographers, this site features a few postcard publishers who produced local views but who were based elsewhere.

Getty Trust
www.getty.edu/research/conducting_research/vocabularies/ulan

The online directory of artists includes British photographers. The search facility sometimes offers back little more than the name it was given. On occasion, however, it can produce a very informative entry.

High street photographers in Aberystwyth, 1857-c1900
www.genuki.org.uk/big/wal/AberPhotos.html

Written by Elizabeth S Darlington, this article originally appeared in the *National Library of Wales Journal*, volume 25, number 4, winter 1988.

History of art: history of photography
www.all-art.org/20ct_photo/20century_photo1.htm

A smattering of studio photographers (generally the best known) can be found among the luminaries featured on this site.

History of photography from its beginnings till the 1920s
www.rleggat.com/photohistory/index.html

Robert Leggatt's site includes articles on a number of photographers, some of them studio professionals. They are generally familiar and frequently noticed figures.

History of photography in Brighton
www.spartacus.schoolnet.co.uk/DShistoryindex.htm

The article forms an accompaniment to a directory of the town's photographers.

International photography hall of fame
http://iphf.org/Hall_Of_Fame/Inductees.html

The title says it all. Fame – as a pioneer, as a technical innovator or as an artist – is the qualification for inclusion. Studio photographers are rarely listed and more rarely British.

John Chillingworth: 20th century greats
www.johnchillingworth.co.uk/words_20cg.html

Most of the photographers discussed on this site are too modern to meet the pre-1920 criterion of this book, but there are a few exceptions.

Luminous Lint
www.luminous-lint.com/app/home/P1

The primary concern of this site is art photography – worldwide and of all periods. A few British studio photographers are included and, since the site is searchable, nothing is lost by feeding in a name. If there is a positive result, it will give links to other web sources for the photographer in question.

Nineteenth century photography
www.paulfrecker.com/home.cfm?pagetype=home

The primary purpose of Paul Frecker's site is selling photographs to collectors. But useful career information is sometimes given about those who took the pictures offered for sale.

Palmquist collection: women in photography
http://beinecke.library.yale.edu/palmquist_wip

The late Peter Palmquist's extensive collection is now housed at Yale University's Beinecke Rare Book and Manuscript Library. Despite an emphasis on the west of the USA, coverage is worldwide, and some British women are included. The search facility seems, at the time of writing, reluctant to divulge information. But it's hoped that the site will eventually allow productive searches for named women photographers.

Photographers of Great Britain and Ireland 1840-1940
www.cartedevisite.co.uk/category/photographers

Ron Cosens' website has already been mentioned in the chapter on 'Directories of early photographers', but this page of his site offers links to a growing number of free biographies.

Photo histories: the photographer's history of photography
www.photohistories.com

So far there has been one relevant article (about Robert Howlett) in this online journal, and that is mentioned in the 'Single studio sources' of this chapter. But the journal is a relatively new venture, and it will be interesting to see how it develops.

PhotoLondon
www.photolondon.org.uk

This database of nineteenth century photographers and allied trades in London has already been mentioned as an online directory, but it offers a wealth of career & biographical information too.

Pre-war photographers in Blackpool & the Fylde area
www.amounderness.co.uk/blackpool_photos_and_photographers.html

The site features articles and photographs relating to a number of Lancashire photographers.

Professional photography in Sussex from 1841 to 1855
www.photohistory-sussex.co.uk/Sussexearly.htm

An article on the county's earliest studios, which is just one of the many pages of interest on the Sussex Photohistory website.

RCS photographers index
www.lib.cam.ac.uk/rcs_photographers/index.html

This biographical index covers photographers known to have taken images in the Royal Commonwealth Society's photograph collection. Some of the entries are very detailed, and many studio photographers are included. The index is useful for non-British Commonwealth photographers and for British photographers who travelled widely or who spent at least part of a career overseas. The qualification for inclusion, however, is the presence of photographs in the collection rather than the mileage achieved by the practitioner. So some sedentary photographers are also represented.

Roger Vaughan's contributors' pages
www.cartes.fsnet.co.uk/index.htm

This page has links to notes (supplied by the website's users) on Charles J Farlie, Joseph Buckley and Emilian Fehrenbach. Other photographers – featured on other pages of Roger Vaughan's several websites – are listed under 'Single studio sources'.

Sharing Wycombe's Old Photographs (SWOP)
www.buckscc.gov.uk/bcc/swop/about.page?

The site has articles on three individual High Wycombe businesses, though only the studio of the Sweetland family dates back to the nineteenth century. But other early photographers are mentioned in two useful articles: *Early professional photographers in Wycombe 1860-1877* and *Early professional photographers in Wycombe 1877-1905*.

Tonbridge history: Some early Tonbridge photographers
www.tonbridgehistory.org.uk/people/tonbridge-photographers.htm

Around a dozen local photographers are referred to, though some are treated in rather less detail than others.

Victorian photography & photographers in Matlock & Matlock Bath
http://freepages.genealogy.rootsweb.ancestry.com/~brett/photos/matlock_photos.html

An essay by John Bradley to accompany Brett Payne's website, listed above.

Who's who of Victorian cinema
www.victorian-cinema.net/whoswho.htm

This site covers pioneers of the cinema, some of whom (including Arthur Albert Collings, William Friese Greene and Eadweard Muybridge) began careers in studio and commercial photography.

Wikipedia
http://en.wikipedia.org/wiki/List_of_photographers

This list of photographers featured in Wikipedia includes some studio professionals (generally the most famous). Researchers will decide for themselves how much reliance to place on Wikipedia articles.

Wolverhampton history and heritage
1. www.localhistory.scit.wlv.ac.uk/articles/photos/earliest.htm

An article on Wolverhampton's earliest photographers by Frank Sharman, with contributions from David Simkin.

2. www.localhistory.scit.wlv.ac.uk/articles/photos/photos02.htm

An article by Frank Sharman on other early photographic studios in Wolverhampton

World history of art: history of photography
www.all-art.org/history658_photography.html

A few early studios (but only the most eminent) are included in the site's dictionary of photographers.

CHAPTER SIX
Periodicals and serial publications

There are a number of photographic journals (and one non-photographic journal) that may be of interest to researchers. But many will think twice about the expense of joining the relevant organisation or subscribing to the journal in question. It is therefore worth checking other options.

The British Library's holdings are as extensive as one might expect. If a visit is intended, it is vital to check whether the St Pancras site or the Colindale site is appropriate, since serial publications are not all held at one location. Personal searching allows browsing opportunities that online searching must generally forgo, but for those unable to visit, the Library operates a document supply service. There is also the possibility of securing a copy of an article through inter-library loan. Researchers should, however, be prepared to pay both processing and copyright fees. The British Library catalogue can be searched online at http://catalogue.bl.uk/F/?func=file&file_name=login-bl-list; information about ordering documents can be found at www.bl.uk/reshelp/atyourdesk/docsupply/index.html; and further advice can be sought by calling 01937 546060 or by e-mailing customer-services@bl.uk.

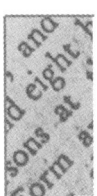

Extensive collections of photographic journals are also in the care of Birmingham Central Library. Their holdings include complete runs of *The Photographic Journal*, *The British Journal of Photography*, the *Almanac* and *The History of Photography*.

It should mentioned, too, that a number of volumes of early photographic journals have been placed on the Google Books website at http://books.google.com. 'Photography' is one of the menu options, but that will produce a huge and unwieldy list of titles. Offering the search engine a specific journal title or a phrase like 'nineteenth century photography' will prove more rewarding.

Where other possible sources of information about photographic journals have been identified, they are mentioned in the individual entries.

Amateur Photographer
(London: IPC Media)

First published in 1884, this title was merged with *Photographic News* in 1908 to form *Amateur Photographer and Photographic News*. Its early terms of reference were not exclusively amateur, and one editor in particular (Alfred Hinton, 1893-1908) pursued a policy of commissioning articles from art photographers and studio photographers.

The British Journal of Photography
(London: Henry Greenwood & Co)

Established in 1854, this periodical began life as *The Liverpool Photographic Journal* and became, in turn, *The Liverpool and Manchester Photographic Journal* and *The Photographic Journal*. As *The Photographic Journal* it became the official organ of almost all the nation's photographic societies. It eventually took the name of *The British Journal of Photography* in 1860. It still appears, but its main emphasis is on current photography. It is, therefore, the earlier issues and incarnations that are likely to be of most interest to researchers.

A fragmentary but very useful collection of issues from the 1870s to the early 1920s can be found at Internet Archives (www.archive.org) by typing 'British Journal of Photography' into the search engine. There are articles on technical aspects of photography, records of applications for patents, and reports on meetings of photographic societies. The last of these categories is potentially useful, since early photographic societies often attracted both amateur and professional members. The issue for 14th January 1887, for instance, gives accounts of meetings of the

Photographic Society of Great Britain, the London and Provincial Photographic Association, the South London Photographic Society, the Glossop Dale Photographic Society and the Dundee and East of Scotland Photographic Association. The following week's issue gave column space to groups from Birkenhead, Birmingham, Sheffield, Yorkshire College, Cardiff and Ireland. These reports abound in names. Whilst the subject and author indexes of the original bound volumes are included, there is no electronic search engine, so it can be time-consuming to locate relevant items. Checking individual names within a potentially interesting report only adds to the arduousness of the task. But many photographers, both amateur and professional, are referred to in these pages.

The British Journal Photographic Almanac Photographer's Daily Companion
(Liverpool: Greenwood)

This early annual is of interest mainly for the light it sheds (via articles and copious advertisements) on day-to-day practice in a photographer's studio. The 1898 and 1910 editions are available at Internet Archives (www.archive.org). It is a work for browsing and absorbing background rather than a source for names.

The History of Photography
(London: Taylor & Francis)

This international quarterly addresses the history, practice and theory of photography. Papers relating to studio photography are not common, but researchers can check for themselves the contents of the more recent editions, which are listed at www.informaworld.com/smpp/title~content=t714595773~db=all~tab=jdb_table_of_contents_previous. *The History of Photography* is also abstracted and indexed in the British Humanities Index and the Periodicals Index Online. (Advice on searching these and similar indexes should be available at any central or academic library, and branch libraries now generally have access to the resources of central libraries.)

Image
(Rochester, New York: International Museum of Photography at George Eastman House)

The journal of the International Museum of Photography includes only occasional articles on British photographers. The journal is, however, searchable by keywords online at http://image.eastmanhouse.org, so nothing is lost by entering a target name. *Image* is also a good source for articles on early photographic processes.

The London Gazette
(London: Stationery Office)

Though not a photographic journal, the *London Gazette* takes note of photographers in a number of ways. Bankruptcies, royal warrants, patent applications, exhibitions and the forming and dissolving of partnerships all find a place in its pages. Coverage is not restricted to the capital.

The London publication is fully online and searchable (with no charge) at www.london-gazette.co.uk, and the home page offers direct links to the Edinburgh and Belfast equivalents. (The *Belfast Gazette* was not published until 1921, but the earlier *Dublin Gazette* can be searched at www.irisoifigiuil.ie.)

Further mention of the Gazettes will be found in the chapter devoted to exhibitions.

The Photogram
(London: Dawbarn & Ward)

Published from 1894 to the end of 1905 (and subsequently under a slightly different title), this monthly journal was accompanied by illustrated supplements and by an annual publication, *Photograms of the Year*, which included exhibition reviews. Some editions of the annual can be found online at:
http://openlibrary.org/books/OL7026291M/Photograms_of_the_year
and at www.archive.org/details/1916photogramsof00londuoft

The Photographic Collector
(London: Bishopsgate Press)

This twice-yearly magazine flourished briefly in the 1980s, and the British Library holds the series. Second-hand copies can sometimes be found, and acquaintance with them suggests that articles of potential interest were sometimes included. But I have found no evidence of any contents list or index to act as a finding aid.

The Photographic News
(London: Cassell, Petter & Galpin)

Established in 1859, this weekly publication was merged with *Amateur Photographer* in 1908 to form *Amateur Photographer and Photographic News*. References to (and writings by) studio professionals are not uncommon, and the magazine is a potentially valuable source. The British Library holdings are complete except for one issue.

The 1875 volume, complete with its original index, can be read online at www.archive.org/details/photographicnew02unkngoog.

Photographica World
(Bushey: The Photographic Collectors Club of Great Britain)

The main focus of this publication is collectable items: cameras, equipment and photographs. But some articles have been devoted to studio photographers and aspects of their work. A two-part index (1977-1997 and 1998 onwards) can be consulted online at www.nanites.co.uk/pccgb/pw%20index%2001.htm. Copies of articles can be bought only by members.

The PhotoHistorian
(Bath: Royal Photographic Society)

This quarterly journal of the Historical Group of the RPS has also been accompanied over the years by a number of supplements, many of which appear in the list of printed photographer directories earlier in this book. Since studio photographers figure prominently among the group's interests, its journal is worth some investigation. An index on the society's website (at www.rps.org/group/Historical/PhotoHistorian-Index) covers the years 1987-1996. Though organised by author, it's brief enough to make scanning the titles quite manageable. The index page also has a link to a list of currently available *PhotoHistorian* Supplements.

PhotoResearcher
(Croydon: European Society for the History of Photography)

Launched in 1990, this journal is published twice a year. Contents lists from issue 1 onwards can be found at www.donau-uni.ac.at/en/department/bildwissenschaft/partnerlinks/eshph/09767/index.php, and all but the most recent issues can be downloaded, in English, from this web page. (The generosity of this gesture deserves to be recognised.) The journal is international in its interests and frequently goes beyond the likely concerns of most single-studio researchers, but the contents lists are worth checking.

Studies in Photography
(Edinburgh: Scottish Society for the History of Photography)

Studies in Photography was known from 1986 to 1995 as *The Scottish Photography Bulletin*. The important Scottish tradition of the pioneering amateur gentleman is strongly reflected in the coverage, but there are also articles on professional photographers.

A full contents list for both titles, and an index (arranged by author), can be found at www.sshop.org.uk/html/publications.htm#index. Some back numbers are still available, though not necessarily to non-members. (The society can be contacted at enquiries@sshop.org.uk .) The British Library holds the *Scottish Photography Bulletin* from 1988 to 1995 and *Studies in Photography* from 1996 to the present.

CHAPTER SEVEN
Photographic societies

The modern perception of a camera club or photographic society is probably of a largely amateur organisation that brings together devotees of a shared hobby. But the nineteenth-century photographic society was rather different. Enthusiasm was no less a qualification, but the distinction between amateur and professional was often less important. Whether photography was a business venture or a leisured pursuit was not always the most important issue. Professional did not necessarily scorn amateur. Both were able chemists and both had creative vision. What mattered was taking photography seriously and believing in its value. There was frequent Victorian discussion of whether photography was an art, and its practitioners were united in the desire to raise its status. Their detractors might think they were slavishly following chemical recipes and exercising routinely acquired manual dexterity. But photographers set a higher value on their activity.

The mixture of amateurs and professionals means that records of photographic interest groups in the nineteenth century can be worth investigating. Some clubs will, of course, have had less professional input than others. But there's a reasonable chance that a studio-running ancestor will have joined a local group and played an active role in its affairs. In the years up to 1900, for example, six of the Edinburgh Photographic Society's twenty presidents were professionals, as were five of its sixteen secretaries.

What's more, the surviving records may go beyond mere lists of office holders. They show, for instance, that James Tunny gave lectures to the Edinburgh society on nine occasions between 1865 and 1885, that he set up a demonstration of carbon printing, and that he tested competing brands of solution for strengthening the density of negatives.

Mixed membership became, however, less characteristic of twentieth century societies. Photography came within the financial reach of the common man. The Box Brownie cost a mere five shillings and required absolutely no skill. The user pointed the camera in the desired direction, pressed the button (or pulled the string), and Kodak did the rest. So there quickly arose a category of amateur who knew nothing of developing and printing and who cared nothing for lighting or composition. It's easy to see how this revolution could have played its part in changing the make-up of photographic societies. One purpose of a club, it can be argued, is to assert (by inclusion or exclusion) the identity that a shared interest can give. But this time, it was not the unbelievers - those who denied the artistic merit of photography - who were excluded. It was rather the mistaken believers - those who presumptuously thought that they too were photographers. So societies came to distinguish between amateur and amateurish. Seriousness of intent still mattered, but the agendas of amateur and professional had diverged. The dedicated hobbyists may have desired to distinguish themselves from the point-and-click brigade, while the high-street businessmen, now in a well-established occupation, may have felt a less acute need for allies in promoting their status. In addition, the rise of the amateur (whatever his level of skill) could be seen as holding potentially disturbing implications for the professional market.

It is for this reason that a fairly arbitrary cut-off point has been set for the discussion here of society and club archives. Records that began before 1900 are included, because there is a reasonable chance of finding evidence of professional photographers among them. Those beginning after 1900 seem generally less likely to repay the effort of investigation, so they are considered in rather less detail.

The first list gives details of those records of early societies that I have been able to locate in repositories. Entries adhere to the sequence: title, scope, location and contact details. Societies have not been included if, by their title, they proclaimed themselves exclusively amateur.

Birmingham Photographic Society
Records, including council and general meeting minute books: c1860-1990.
Birmingham Archives and Heritage Service, Floor 6, Central Library, Chamberlain Square, Birmingham | Tel: 0121 303 4549.
www.birmingham.gov.uk/cs/Satellite/localstudieslibrary?packedargs=website%3D1&rendermode=live

Borough Polytechnic Photographic Society
Minutes: 1895-1973.
John Harvard Library, 211 Borough High Street, London, SE1 1JA.
Tel: 020 7525 20000 | www.southwark.gov.uk/info/200161/local_history_library

Bristol Photographic Society
Photographs and records (17 boxes): c1890s-2006.
Bristol Record Office, 'B' Bond Warehouse, Smeaton Road, Bristol, BS1 6XN.
Tel: 0117 922 4224 | www.bristol.gov.uk/ccm/navigation/leisure-and-culture/records-and-archives

Chester Photographic Society
Minutes: 1887-1905.
Cheshire Archives & Local Studies, Duke Street, Chester, CH1 1RL.
Tel: 01244 972574 | www.cheshireeast.gov.uk/recordoffice

Chichester Camera Club
Records: 1896-1982.
West Sussex Record Office, Sherburne House, 3 Orchard Street, Chichester, PO19 1RN (correspondence to: County Hall, Chichester, PO19 1RN) | Tel: 01243 753602.
www.westsussex.gov.uk/leisure/explore_west_sussex/record_office_and_archives/about_us_location_opening_ho.aspx

Croydon Camera Club
Photographs, calendars, catalogues, photographs and more: 1890 onward.
Central Library, Croydon Clocktower, Katharine Street, Croydon, CR9 1ET
Tel: 020 8726 6900 | www.croydon.gov.uk/leisure/libraries/croydonlibs/centrallib

Dukinfield Photographic Society
1. Scrapbook: 1888-1913.
2. Records: 1891-1963.
Tameside Local Studies & Archives, Tameside Central Library, Old Street, Ashton-under-Lyne, OL6 7SG | Tel: 0161 342 4242.
www.tameside.gov.uk/localstudies

Edinburgh Photographic Society
Record of meetings, transactions, outings, membership and more: 1866-2000.
The Edinburgh Room, Edinburgh Central Library, 9 George IV Bridge, Edinburgh, EH1 1EG | Tel: 0131 242 8030.
www.edinburgh.gov.uk/directory_record/5083/edinburgh_room
(Much of the information from these documents can also be found online at www.edinphoto.org.uk/4/4__eps.htm.)

Hackney Photographic Society
Minutes, accounts, membership records: 1858-1989.
Hackney Archives Department, 43 De Beauvoir Road, London, N1 5SQ.
Tel: 020 7241 2886 | www.hackney.gov.uk/ca-archives.htm

Huddersfield Naturalist, Photographic and Antiquarian Society
Minutes and papers: 1881-1966.
West Yorkshire Archive Service, Kirklees Central Library, Princess Alexandra Walk, Huddersfield, HD1 2SU | Tel: 01484 221966.
www.archives.wyjs.org.uk/wyjs-archives-kirklees.asp

Kingston Camera Club
Minutes, membership records, financial records and other papers: 1894-1993.
Kingston Museum & Heritage Service, North Kingston Centre, Richmond Road, Kingston-upon-Thames, KT2 5PE.
Tel: 020 8547 6738 | www.kingston.gov.uk/museums

Leeds Photographic Society
Minute books, correspondence, financial records and more: 1853-2003.
West Yorkshire Archives Service, 2 Chapeltown Road, Sheepscar, Leeds, LS7 3AP.
Tel: 0113 214 5814 | www.archives.wyjs.org.uk/wyjs-archives-leeds.asp

Leicester and Leicestershire Photographic Society
1. Records: 1883-1991.
2. Photographs: c1870-1929.
Leicestershire, Leicester & Rutland Record Office, Long Street, Wigston Magma, Leicester, LE18 2AH | Tel: 0116 257 1080 | www.leics.gov.uk/index/community/museums/record_office.htm

Lewes Photographic Society
Minutes, attendance register and list of members: 1888-1994.
East Sussex Record Office, The Maltings, Castle Precincts, Lewes, BN7 1YT.
Tel: 01273 482349 | www.eastsussex.gov.uk/useourarchives

Manchester Photographic Society
Minutes, membership records, activities, correspondence and more: 1855-1976.
Greater Manchester County Record Office (with Manchester Archives), 56 Marshall Street, New Cross, Manchester, M4 5FU | Tel: 0161 832 5284.
www.gmcro.co.uk

Nottingham and Nottinghamshire Photographic Society
Minutes, membership lists, correspondence, newsletters, programmes, annual reports, press cuttings and other records: 1892-1992.
Nottinghamshire Archives, County House, Castle Meadow Road, Nottingham, NG2 1AG | Tel: 0115 958 1634 | www.nottinghamshire.gov.uk/archives

Oldham Photographic Society
Minutes, account books, letter books, historical survey committee minutes (1910-11), syllabuses, exhibition records and society history: 1867-1968.
Greater Manchester County Record Office (with Manchester Archives), 56 Marshall Street, New Cross, Manchester, M4 5FU | Tel: 0161 832 5284 | www.gmcro.co.uk

Oxford Camera Club
Minutes and papers: 1894 1915.
Oxford University, Bodleian Library, Special Collections and Western Manuscripts, Broad Street, Oxford, OX1 3BG.
Tel: 01865 277158 | www.bodley.ox.ac.uk/dept/scwmss

Oxford Photographic Society
Minutes: 1889-1891.
Oxford University, Bodleian Library, Special Collections and Western Manuscripts, Broad Street, Oxford, OX1 3BG.
Tel: 01865 277158 | www.bodley.ox.ac.uk/dept/scwmss

Photographic Society of Scotland
Minutes, correspondence, papers relating to exhibitions, etc: 1856-1873.
National Archives of Scotland, HM General Register House, Edinburgh, EH1 3YY.
Tel: 0131 535 1334 | www.nas.gov.uk
(Much information derived from these records can also be found at www.edinphoto.org.uk/3__pss.htm#Exhibitions.)

Stockport Photographic Society
Scrapbook (members' work rather than society documents): late 1890s/early 1900s.
Stockport Central Heritage Library, Wellington Road South, Stockport, SK1 3RS.
Tel: 0161 474 4530 | www.stockport.gov.uk/services/leisureculture/libraries/yourlibrary/yourlocallibrary/centralheritagelibrary2

West Kent Natural History, Microscopical and Photographic Society
1. Annual reports: 1880s/1890s.
Bexley Local Studies and Archive Centre, Central Library, Townley Road,

Bexleyheath, DA6 7HJ | Tel: 0208 836 7369 | http://archives.bexley.gov.uk
2. Attendance book: 1881-1914; minute book: 1891-1913.
Greenwich Heritage Centre, Artillery Square, Royal Arsenal, Woolwich, SE18 4DX.
Tel: 020 8854 2452 | www.greenwich.gov.uk/Greenwich/LeisureCulture/History
AndHeritage/HeritageCentre/HeritageCentre.htm

Researchers are also reminded of the Royal Photographic Society (originally the Photographic Society of London). Its archives are lodged with the National Media Museum, and records of its proceedings are to be found in the *British Journal of Photography* (which, in its earlier incarnations, was the organ of record for almost all of the pioneer photographic societies). More information on these sources can be found in the chapters on 'Material in archives' and 'Periodicals and serial publications'.

These same sources are also worth checking when no other evidence of a known society can be found, when a society's surviving archive begins at a surprisingly late date, or when a society's existence has not been continuous. A number of groups began life in the 1850s and early 1860s, but foundered fairly quickly. Sometimes they were later resurrected under the same or a slightly different title. The records of the Norwich Photographic Society serve to illustrate this. The society was founded in 1854, enjoyed a vigorous life for seven years, and was then disbanded. In 1903 a new society was formed, and this has survived to the present day. Reports of the old group's meetings were preserved in the archives of the Royal Photographic Society, while records of the reborn club found their way to the Norfolk Record Office.

A number of these early societies are described on Peter Stubbs' EdinPhoto website, which gives dates of establishment, arrangements for meetings, an A-Z of office holders and the names of some other committee members. The initial page is www.edinphoto.org.uk/1_early/1_early_photography_-_societies_-_background.htm. Some of these groups have already been mentioned. The others are listed below in alphabetical order of location rather than title, with dates of foundation in brackets.

Photographic Society of Belfast (1857)
Blackheath Photographic Society (1857)
Bradford Photographic Society (1860)
Brighton and Sussex Photographic Society (1855)
Chorlton Photographic Association (1857)
Devon and Cornwall Photographic Society (1854)
Dublin Photographic Society (1854)

Dumfries and Galloway Photographic Society (1856)
City of Glasgow and West of Scotland Photographic Association (1860)
Greenwich Photographic Society (1857)
Liverpool Photographic Society (1853)
Macclesfield Photographic Society (1858)
Newcastle on Tyne Photographic Society (1861)
North London Photographic Association (1857)
Nottingham Photographic Society (1858)
Paisley Photographic Society (1857)
South London Photographic Society (1859)

It could be argued that the criterion of a pre-1900 start to society records is too uncompromising. After all, professional photographers did not suddenly and with one accord resign from societies just because a new century had started. Researchers taking this view will wish to check the holdings of appropriate local archives, and will also consider whether the National Register of Archives (www.nationalarchives.gov.uk/nra/default.asp) can offer a short cut to promising sources. (Search in the 'corporate name' category, trying both 'photographic society' and 'camera club'.) It is with these researchers in mind that a further brief list is given of new or revived groups whose surviving archived records began between 1900 and 1920.

Acton Photographic Society (1904ff); Ealing Local History Centre
Bedford Camera Club (1906ff); Bedfordshire & Luton Archives
Belfast Camera Club (1912ff); Public Record Office, Northern Ireland
Brighton & Hove Camera Club (1900ff); East Sussex Record Office
Cardiff Camera Club (1906ff); Glamorgan Archives
Durham Photographic Society (1911ff); Durham County Record Office
Halifax Photographic Society (1901ff); West Yorkshire Archive Service, Calderdale
Hampshire House Photographic Society (1911ff), Hammersmith & Fulham Archives
Lancashire and Cheshire Photographic Union (1905ff), Greater Manchester County Record Office
Newcastle Photographic Society (1919ff); Tyne & Wear Archives Service
North Wilts Field & Camera Club (1904ff); Swindon Central Library
Norwich & District Photographic Society (1903ff); Norfolk Record Office
Stafford Photographic Society (1907ff); Staffordshire Record Office
Wolverhampton Photographic Society (1902ff); Centre for Birmingham Studies

One final thought is offered, though it is no more than an unexplored speculation. Researchers looking into photographic societies may well find evidence of groups with 'Amateur' in the title. These, ostensibly, are of no interest to those seeking information about professionals, so they have been excluded from this chapter. But there seems no reason why an amateur club should not, from time to time, have called on a professional to give a lecture or conduct a demonstration.

CHAPTER EIGHT
Exhibitions

Many studio professionals submitted their work to photographic exhibitions or to exhibitions of industry and the arts. As well as being personally gratifying, success - measured in terms of prizes won or medals awarded - could be good for business.

The first exhibition of photographs in Britain could be said to be the 'photogenic drawings' shown by William Henry Fox Talbot to the British Association in Birmingham in August 1839. Other displays followed, and these were usually small and often devoted to the work of one practitioner. But a much larger body of images, from home and abroad, was offered to public view at the Great Exhibition of 1851. Then came the first major exhibition devoted solely to photographs, which was mounted the following year at London's Society of Arts, and this served as a spur to the formation of the Photographic Society in 1853. Thereafter the tradition of public display became firmly established: the appearance of photographs (and photographic equipment) in both dedicated and more general exhibitions was a fact of national and international life.

Happily, information about some of these exhibitions has survived, and in certain cases the record of contributors and their images is quite detailed. Photographic society records and photographic journals are worth checking, where there's an event of known locality or year to investigate,

but there are some other very accessible sources that can also be investigated. Three of these are particularly worth exploring.

Early photographic exhibitions in Britain

This source first appeared in book form:

Taylor, Roger, *Photographs exhibited in Britain, 1839-1865* (Ottawa: National Gallery of Canada, 2002).

It provides a brief overview of the background to early exhibitions and photographic societies, and it goes on to list the photographers, photographs exhibited and processes used, as published in the original catalogues. Both the British Library and the Guildhall Library have a copy of this book, as well as a copy of one of the catalogues on which it draws:

International Exhibition, London 1862, *Catalogue of the photographs exhibited in Class XIV* (London: Her Majesty's Commissioners, 1862).

But the information from Taylor's book has now been made available online at http://peib.dmu.ac.uk/index.php. This website, *Photographic Exhibitions in Britain 1839-1865*, is hosted by De Montfort University and contains individual records for over 20,000 exhibits from over 40 catalogues. It is searchable by exhibition, photographer, process and price, and it gives the locations of the catalogues that were used to compile the information.

Exhibitions of the Royal Photographic Society

Also hosted by De Montfort University, *Exhibitions of the Royal Photographic Society 1870-1915* is a website that can be found at http://erps.dmu.ac.uk. It contains over 45,000 records from the annual exhibition catalogues of the Photographic Society of London. Information covers exhibits, exhibitors, judges and members of the hanging and selection committees. Catalogue pages are reproduced, complete with such illustrations as were originally included. Additional illustrations and exhibitions reviews from *Photograms of the year* are also made available. The site is searchable by exhibitions, exhibitors, exhibits, judges and catalogue pages.

Exhibitions in Scotland

Peter Stubbs' encyclopaedic EdinPhoto website has already been mentioned in a number of contexts. It also contains a wealth of detail on exhibitions in Scotland (to which, it should be noted, non-Scots also contributed).

Information about exhibitions of the Photographic Society of Scotland, 1856-1866, can be found at www.edinphoto.org.uk/3/3__pss.htm#Exhibitions. The amount of information varies from year to year. At best, it goes beyond the mere naming of medal winners to give an extensive list of exhibitors, and extracts from press reports, letters or other documents are sometimes included.

There is also material relating to exhibitions of the Edinburgh Photographic Society, and this can be discovered at www.edinphoto.org.uk/4/4__eps.htm #EXHIBITIONS. Information relates to Open Exhibitions from 1861 and Members' Exhibitions from 1882, and coverage of both extends into the present century. Once again, the amount of information varies, though there is, in general, less detail than for the national exhibitions. But there is still some valuable material to sift through.

Other sources of information about exhibitions may seem rather slight by comparison with the three already discussed. The following nevertheless have their uses.

University of Glasgow Library

This library holds, in its special collections, documents relating to a number of national and international exhibitions, and some of this material includes information about photographic content. London 1862, Vienna 1873, Paris 1878 and Paris 1889 are among the exhibitions included, and more information can be found at http://special.lib.gla.ac.uk/teach/century/designreform.html#resource %20listing . (Website redesign was in progress at the time of writing, so this address may become obsolete.) Advice should be sought before a visit is considered, and the contact details are: Library, University of Glasgow, Hillhead Street, Glasgow G12 8QE, Scotland. Tel: 0141 330 6704.

The London Gazette

As indicated in the chapter on periodicals and serial publications, the *London Gazette* (and its Scottish and Irish counterparts) can provide some useful information about photographers. This includes reference to exhibitions of trade and industry, both in Britain and overseas. In some cases, there is a list of exhibitors and medals; in others, the details are restricted to the announcement of categories, judging panels and regulations for submission. A specific event can be looked up, if it is already known from other sources that a photographer showed work there. Otherwise, it is probably best to type a photographer's name into the search engine and invite it to sort results by the 'earliest first' criterion. (Items from the pre-photographic era may well be offered, but relevant entries will still be identified more quickly than if recent records are given priority.)

Lists of exhibitions and world fairs

The hungry researcher may find only meagre nourishment at www.fact-index.com/l/li/list_of_world_s_fairs.html, which is simply a list of international fairs and exhibitions from the 1750s to the present. Many of the listed events fall outside the relevant period, and photography was not represented at all those events that did occur within its lifetime. Where, however, it is already known (perhaps from a photographic mount) that a professional exhibited at a specific event, the site can sometimes lead to a little background information. The list is full of links, most of which are merely to sites focusing on the exhibition's host city. But there are some links that lead to background information about the exhibition itself. (A similar list is located at http://en.wikipedia.org/wiki/List_of_world's_fairs.)

More useful may be the list of national and international exhibitions covered by collections in the Science Museum Library. This is to be found at www.sciencemuseum.org.uk/sitecore/shell/Controls/Rich%20Text%20Editor/~/media/315F317C49574EF5AE2285B3A8CF06B9.ashx. Photography is, of course, just one of many possible subject areas referred to in these holdings. So, while the library and archives are open for public use, it is important to make a preliminary approach and seek advice. Contact details are: Science Museum Library, Imperial College Road, South Kensington, London, SW7 5NH. Tel: 020 7942 4242.

CHAPTER NINE
Visiting

Recommending days out for photographic historians goes rather beyond the remit of this book. The reader is therefore invited to set imaginary parentheses around this very brief chapter, and it is with some diffidence that I draw attention to a small handful of places of interest. It is important to check opening hours in advance, particularly since there can be significant seasonal variations.

The first two locations are the nearest thing there is, photographically speaking, to required visiting.

The National Media Museum
Bradford, West Yorkshire, BD1 1NQ | Tel: 0844 856 3797.
www.nationalmediamuseum.org.uk

The museum has already been mentioned for the archives it holds, but it is also worth visiting as a tourist attraction. Photographic material can be found in many museums, but none has a collection to approach the one at Bradford.

Fox Talbot Museum, Lacock Abbey
Lacock, near Chippenham, Wiltshire SN15 2LG | Tel: 01249 730459.
www.nationaltrust.org.uk/main/w-vh/w-visits/w-findaplace/w-lacockabbeyvillage/
w-lacockabbeyvillage-talbotmuseum.htm

The Fox Talbot archive is now housed at the British Library, but the museum and home can still be visited. The photographer was a gentleman amateur, and licensing requirements put his calotype process generally beyond the reach of professionals; but it would be a hard-hearted researcher who declined to be interested in a figure of such monumental importance.

The next two places might be viewed much as Dr Johnson viewed the Giant's Causeway. ('Worth seeing, yes; but not worth going to see.') It would be a pity to visit the Isle of Wight or North Yorkshire and miss them.

Dimbola Lodge Museum
The Julia Margaret Cameron Trust, Terrace Lane, Freshwater Bay, Isle of Wight, PO40 9QE | Tel: 01983 756814; www.dimbola.co.uk

Rescued from demolition at the eleventh hour, Julia Margaret Cameron's home now houses (among other attractions) a permanent exhibition of her work. Her world, like Talbot's, is far from that of the studio professional, but her images are worth studying.

The Sutcliffe Gallery
1 Flowergate, Whitby; YO21 3BA | Tel: 01947 602239.
www.sutcliffe-gallery.co.uk

It's a shop. But where else can one go into a shop and be surrounded by the memorable images of a single studio photographer?

The final recommendations focus very firmly on the professional photographer's world. Here and there, the building that housed an early studio can be pointed out; and here and there, a north-facing window or skylight remains. But the survival of a whole studio, entire of itself, is very rare indeed. These are the two that I know of.

William Hayes' studio
Ryedale Folk Museum, Hutton-le-Hole, York, YO62 6UA | Tel: 01751 417 367.
www.ryedalefolkmuseum.co.uk

Hayes' very simple studio was originally built in his York garden in 1902. In 1911 it was taken down and re-erected on a new site at Hutton-le-Hole. In the 1980s it was moved again, but this time over a short distance, to form part of the museum.

Robert Clapperton's studio
The Robert D Clapperton Photographic Trust, 28 Scotts Place, Selkirk, TD7 4DR.
Tel: 01750 20523 | www.selkirk.bordernet.co.uk/rclapperton

This daylight studio was established in 1867 and was used by three generations of the Clapperton family. The premises remain in family ownership and have now been set up as a museum and photographic archive.

CHAPTER TEN
The photographs themselves

Photographs are often the main surviving evidence of a photographer's life and work, and they should not be ignored or written off as peripheral to serious study. The mounts - particularly the informative mounts of cartes de visite and cabinet prints - can provide useful information, and the images they support may also have their own story to tell. Reading that story does, however, pose its own problems. To tackle these, it is often helpful to be familiar with the business of dating and interpreting old photographs. Although systematic exploration of these themes lies outside the scope of this book, the bibliography offers a number of suggestions for appropriate further reading. All that is attempted here is a consideration of the sort of questions that, faced with a photograph or a group of photographs, one can ask oneself.

But photographic images take the researcher into contentious territory, for one man's interpretation is another man's conjecture. At times this chapter will venture onto ground where, some might argue, a scrupulous historian should not tread. Consider, however, the alternative. It was quite common for a photographer to leave behind evidence of his working life on a scale that was impossible for most ancestors; and it would be a missed opportunity to have access to such a body of work without attempting to evaluate it. It is important, of course, to recognise when one is going

beyond documented fact and to know the difference between suggestions and conclusions. So the researcher needs to temper an imaginatively open mind with the critical detachment of scholarly inquiry. That applies to the images produced by a photographic ancestor, and it may also apply to some aspects of this chapter.

1. Finding examples

Clearly, the more examples of a photographer's work can be examined, the better chance there is of making useful observations. Some photographs may have been inherited, and it's always worth checking the remoter reaches of the family to see if anything else has survived. (For some thoughts on exchanging copies, see the 'Talking to relations' section of the 'Conventional sources' chapter.)

Other examples may be found in the collections of local history centres, record offices and museums. Holdings based on specific studios have been discussed in the chapter headed 'Material in archives', but many individual photographs survive in collections relating to locations, events and businesses. Examples of these can sometimes be found online, simply by typing the photographer's name into a search engine. (Unless it's a very uncommon name, it's probably sensible to add 'photographer' and the name of the town to the search terms.) Such searches, incidentally, sometimes produce evidence of a picture for sale.

Then there are the books of old photographs that have been produced for most localities. Many form part of an extensive series, produced by such publishers as Sutton, Batsford and Hendon (to name but some). Others are locally-published labours of love by civic societies, historical groups or enthusiastic individuals. The county, town or village is the object of interest, but the photographs are the work of professionals and amateurs who should be identified in index, credits or captions. Though recent books of this kind are likely to be on sale locally, many older volumes are long out of print. But the Society of Genealogists has a useful collection of such works (as mentioned in the 'Conventional sources' chapter), and local libraries usually hold copies relevant to their area. Remainder bookshops can also sometimes be worth checking.

Finally, there is always the chance of finding old photographs - and studio portraits in particular - at fleamarkets and antique fairs. It is, admittedly, a hit-or-miss procedure (with the main emphasis on 'miss'), but it can sometimes produce results. Dealers often acquire items locally, so there's a stronger chance of finding a photographer's pictures in the town or county where he worked. Many stallholders will display a few handfuls of photographs in a box that has to be sorted through on the off-chance of finding something relevant, but more specialist dealers will have their wares organised into albums and will know what is in them. This may not increase the chance of making a find, but it can make searching rather easier.

2. Photographic mounts

Once some examples of a photographer's work have been found, the process of interrogating them can begin. If those examples include cartes de visite or cabinet prints, then the best place to start is the mount. The cards to which these popular photographic formats were pasted provided the photographer with a perfect opportunity for self-promotion, so the design and text of a mount can often tell us something about the practitioner's products and services and about how he positioned himself in the market.

The most basic information was the photographer's name and address, but other studio information sometimes appeared. Opening times might be given; finding directions might be offered; attention might be drawn to the advent of electricity. It was not uncommon, in an occupation where newcomers often tried their luck, to boast of long experience (either by referring to the number of years spent in the business, or by giving a date of establishment). Such details need, however, to be treated with a little caution. The total of years was sometimes rounded up, and 'established' could be defined in more than one way, as discussion of Figure 3 will shortly show.

A reference to products or services was not uncommon. Some photographers alluded to a process they used, if its adoption was recent, or if it had required the buying of a licence. In the second half of the 1870s, for instance, Vincent Hatch was promoting himself as the sole licensee of the chromotype process in Huddersfield. Some practitioners gave an indication of their prices. The ability to supply copies was frequently mentioned, along with the possibility of coloured or enlarged copies, and a space was often provided for a serial number to locate the negative when copying orders were received. Many such handwritten serial numbers survive, though the day books that recorded their significance have long since disappeared. It is tempting to wonder whether such numbers could give an idea of a photographer's work-rate. This could, in theory, be estimated, if the date of a photograph and the date of the studio's establishment are both known, or if two numbered pictures from the same studio can be dated. But so many variables are possible, that an average figure for sittings per year may not prove very enlightening. Some photographers numbered each image separately, while others assigned numbers to sittings, using letters to designate pictures taken within a sitting. In addition, the output of daylight studios fluctuated considerably: it was affected by weather conditions and by time of year, and summer visitors or market day crowds could affect the evenness of demand. Jasper Wright's King's Lynn studio, for example, attracted an unprecedented 65 customers on 21st January 1899 during the town's annual fair. Later that year, on 1st September, the combination of market day and the end of harvesting brought a healthy 20 sitters to his Swaffham studio in the morning, but the onset of rain killed business later in the day. It is evident, therefore, that work-rate averages, even if they can be attempted, can give only a very crude idea of a studio's trade.

Card mounts also offered professionals space on which to promote an image of themselves and stress what today would be called their 'unique selling point'. In practice, of course, selling points tended to be no more unique then than they generally are now, but they did show how an individual sought to differentiate himself from his local competition. Some aimed to present themselves as artists or (less commonly) scientists. The status of photography was a subject of some debate, and early practitioners often used a design incorporating a palette, say, or an easel, to stress that they were more than rude mechanicals. Others emphasised their civic pride, identifying themselves with the communities they served by depicting the town's coat of arms or a local landmark. Yet others presented themselves as gentlemen and scholars, using quotations or Latin tags, such as the 'Sol fecit' strapline favoured by J R Sawyer of Norwich. Boasting distinguished patrons was a popular option, though some photographers were inclined to suggest a degree of patronage that could not fairly be claimed. ('Photographer to the Queen', accompanied by the royal arms, sometimes implied the holding of a Royal Warrant where none had been granted.) A further form of distinction was conferred by competitive success, so a number of professionals decorated their mounts with reproductions of medals won at national or international exhibitions.

Mounts will sometimes give an indication of a photographer's attempt to occupy a market niche. Among the more common manifestations are the use of Masonic emblems, a professed willingness to undertake out-of-studio work, and a claim to specialise in the portraiture of children. But there were also professionals who aimed at military, scholarly or clerical markets, and the references (already mentioned) to titled patrons can be seen, in part at least, as a bid for the attention of the market's upper segments. Around 1900 William Amey of Landport, Portsmouth, was seeking a clientele among other people's dissatisfied customers. 'People who have never come out well in a photograph are especially invited to give us a sitting as no matter where previously taken, we can insure a successful portrait in any case, without exception.'

Researchers may also wish to consider the overall style of mount design. Popular photographers could find themselves needing new mount stock every six months or so. Often this meant a simple repeat order, but the opportunity was there to review the current design and decide whether a change or improvement was needed. Fashions in mount design evolved over the decades, so, given a familiarity with the skills of photographic dating, it is sometimes possible to determine whether a photographer was in the vanguard of changing tastes or was inclined to lag behind the times. In addition, there is the source of the design to be considered. Major suppliers, such as Marion & Co. and Trapp & Münch, offered stock designs that could be customised with the addition of individual studio details. The results could be impressive, yet some production expense could be saved. Many photographers chose this option, but others had designs drawn up specifically for their own studios. Investigation of mount designs (some help with which is available at www.cartes.freeuk.com/dated/marion.htm) can help the researcher distinguish between professionals who took the relatively easy route and professionals who invested in more ambitious self-presentation.

A very few examples must suffice to illustrate more precisely what can be gleaned from mounts.

Figure 1 shows a Humphreys & Whaite carte de visite mount from the Cheltenham studio they occupied in the second half of the 1860s. Mount design was in its infancy at this time, and the common choice was to fill a fraction of the available space with a simple trade plate. Humphreys & Whaite follow customary practice in broad terms with a scroll-borne name and address surrounded by an expanse of white space. But they go one stage further and their inclusion of small line drawings shows an awareness of graphics' emblematic potential. At the heart of their design is a camera, the symbol of their trade. Above it appears the sun, on which all practitioners depended. But it is the objects on either side of the camera that make a personal statement. To the right is a palette with brushes; to the left is a chemist's pestle and mortar. The photographers are addressing the Victorian debate about the nature of their occupation, and are finding in favour of both sides of the argument. They are presenting themselves as both artists and scientists. We may notice that the camera is a little closer to the palette, and that it points towards it, but we should probably refrain from pushing the interpretation too far. What may be concluded, though, is that Humphreys & Waite are in the vanguard of those exploiting the possibilities of mount design, and that they are demanding that their business should be taken seriously.

Figure 2, another carte mount, also dates from the 1860s and originates from the Lyndhurst studio of J G & E G Short. The all-over back design suggests that they, too, are forward-thinking, for many (probably most) of their competitors will still have been featuring simple trade plates. They draw attention, fairly routinely, to the

Figure 1

UNDER THE PATRONAGE OF
HER MAJESTY & THE ROYAL FAMILY.

Duplicates at any time by sending name.

Figure 2

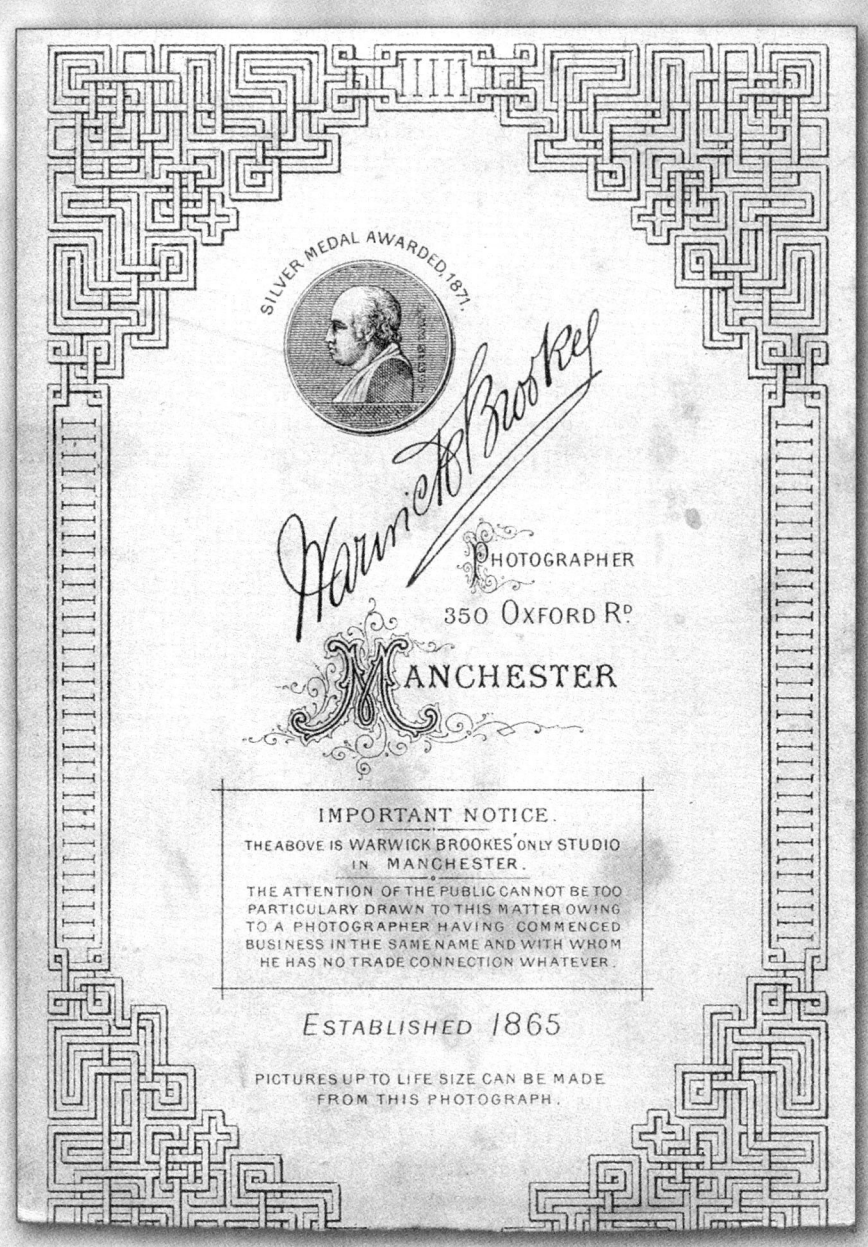

Figure 3

possibility of ordering further copies, and they indulge a taste for varied typefaces that was to become common in the 1870s. Forming an arch at the top of the design are the words: '1st class silver medal and certificate of honor (sic) awarded for photographs of children &c'. With this statement the Shorts manage to tick two promotional boxes at the same time. They draw attention to their achievements in competition (without being precise about occasion or location), and they make a bid to be seen as specialists in child photography. Long exposures and fidgety infants often led to spoilt plates, so many early photographers were reluctant to photograph children, and some imposed an additional charge for doing so. There was, therefore, a possible competitive advantage in being seen to be child-friendly. But it's the coat of arms - accompanied by 'under the patronage of Her Majesty and the Royal Family' - that dominates the design. The Shorts doubtless took some royal pictures, but they were never granted the Royal Warrant that would justify displaying the coat of arms. Like a number of other photographers (until a court case of the early 1880s), they are suggesting a stronger and more official link with royalty than is justifiable. Thus presumption and a lively business sense go hand in hand.

Warwick Brookes was at 350 Oxford Road, Manchester, from the late 1870s, but **Figure 3**, a cabinet print mount, belongs to a period of competition that began in the early 1880s and is referred to in an 'Important notice':

'The above is Warwick Brookes' only studio in Manchester. The attention of the public cannot be too particularly drawn to this matter owing to a photographer having commenced business in the same name and with whom he has no trade connections whatever.'

The offender was Warwick Brookes Junior, and the disclaimer strikes a dramatic note that is rare on mounts. (The problem was not, however, unprecedented. In the 1860s Arthur Nichols of Cambridge, competing with unrelated bearers of the same surname, found it necessary to insist he had 'no connection with any other house'.) But the combative tone should not distract us from other details of Brookes' mount. He offers enlargements up to life size and he gives an establishment date of 1856. This date reminds us of the care needed in the interpretation of such information. It indicates when the photographer first set up a studio, but it applies neither to the business name nor to the address on the mount. Gillian Jones' directory of Lancashire photographers (listed in the 'Directory of early photographers' chapter) shows that Warwick Brookes began his career as part of the W & J Brookes partnership in the mid-1860s and was active at five studios before settling at 350 Oxford Road. The last feature to be noticed is the depiction of an 1871 James Watt silver medal. Photographers regularly contributed to the exhibitions of the Royal Cornwall Polytechnic Society at Falmouth, and those who earned a James Watt medal often recorded this distinction on their mounts.

Samuel A. Walker,
Fine Art Photographer
To The Queen, Bishops & Clergy,
230, Regent Street, W.
opposite Hanover Street,
London.

N.B. PORTRAITS OF LADIES CHILDREN & LAYMEN AS WELL AS THE CLERGY ARE TAKEN DAILY AT THIS STUDIO, ALSO PHOTOGRAPHS OF EVERY DESCRIPTION.

An enlargement can be made at any time from this Negative N°. 13106
All negatives carefully kept.

Figure 4

The carte mount that forms **Figure 4** probably dates from the early 1880s, though Samuel Walker continued at the 230 Regent Street studio until the mid-90s. The finding direction below his address ('opposite Hanover Street') is not superfluous. The sitter for this carte already knows how to find the studio, of course, but cartes were given to friends and family and admired by visitors. There was always a chance, therefore, that a mount would be seen by a potential new customer. Walker makes the common offer of supplying enlargements, and the serial number has been entered in the designated space, thereby reinforcing the assurance of 'All negatives carefully kept'. But not only is he indicating he has a safe pair of hands; he is indicating that they are a distinguished pair of hands. He is a 'fine art' photographer whose clients include queen, bishops and clergy, and he emphasises the point by depicting a mitre and the royal arms (though, like J G & E G Short, he lacks the warrant that would entitle him to display them). It is evident from the mitre and the reference to bishops and clergy that he is promoting himself to a niche market, and the overall tone of the mount exudes a sobriety appropriate to clerical portraiture. Despite the customary variety of fonts, the impression is one of restraint: the illustrations are small; all the text is kept on a straight line; and the swirls, curlicues and general exuberance of Figures 2, 3, 5 and 6 are absent. But though Walker is keen to occupy a niche, he has no wish to be walled up within it, and he reminds us that 'Portraits of ladies children & laymen as well as the clergy are taken daily at this studio, also photographs of every description'.

Studio dating suggests that **Figure 5**, a W & J Stuart cabinet print mount, belongs to the 1890s, though the design had been popular since the mid-1880s. It is one of Trapp & Münch's stock designs and probably originated with them, though copies and near-copies were also produced by other suppliers. The angled name, the bamboo, the fan and the birds were standard elements, and other details could be fitted in to order. The bamboo and fan were an expression of the age's fascination with the oriental, so the Stuarts can be seen as reflecting popular taste rather than pioneering it. But they make the most of the customisable space. The note at the bottom draws attention to a range of services in addition to the straightforward supply of copies. They can reduce images to miniature proportions or enlarge them up to life size, and they can offer a choice of coloured finishes, including oil, watercolours and crayons. They also point out that they have electric lighting. The depiction of a medal for merit, won at the Vienna Exhibition of 1873, is intended to confer added status, as is, presumably, the royal coat of arms. But the coat of arms is a little puzzling, as it is accompanied by no kind of claim or explanation. The aim, it would seem, is distinction by association. Certainly there seems to be no justification for the presence of this detail. A William Slade Stuart was later (in 1896) granted a Royal Warrant as part of the Gunn & Stuart partnership, but he appears to be a different person. What is more, the authority of the royal arms is

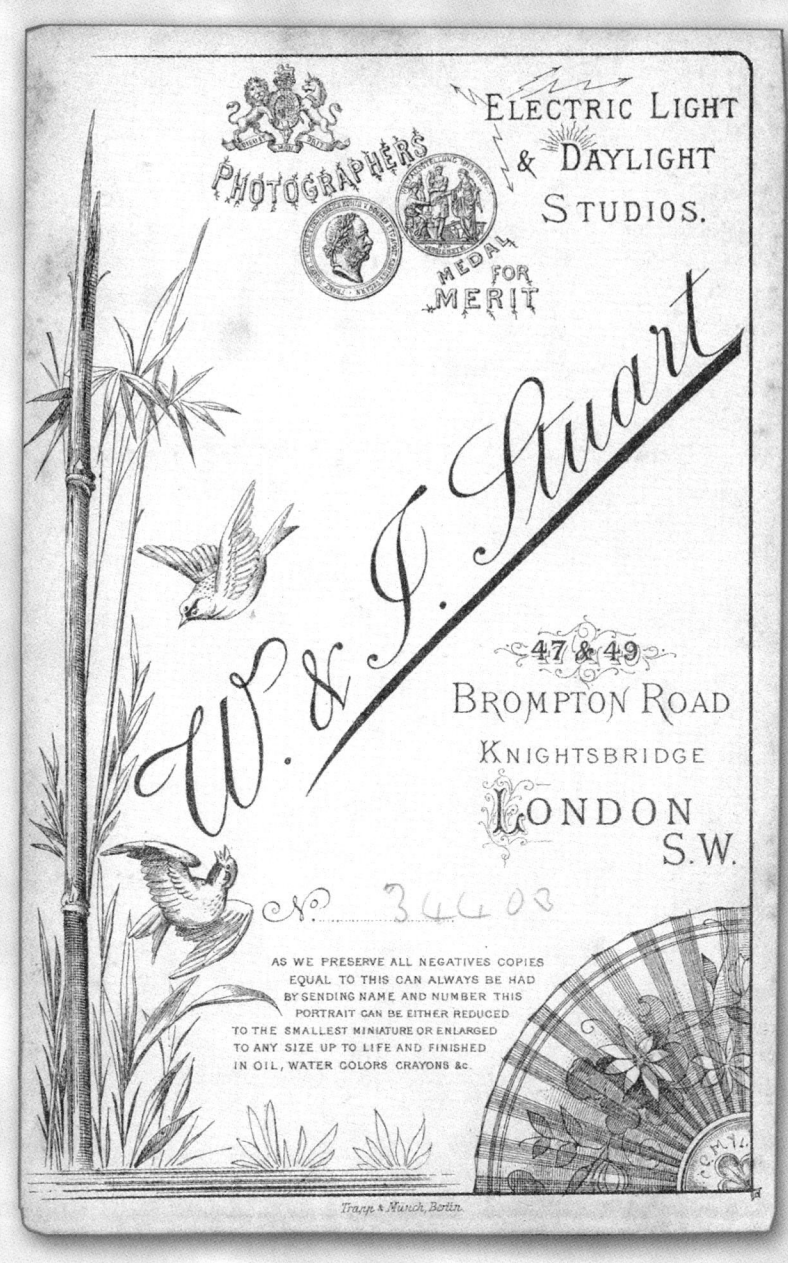

Figure 5

further undermined when, on close inspection, the motto turns out to read 'Dieu et mon drit.'

Figure 6, a carte mount from the 1890s, comes from G P Cartland's studio in Windsor High Street. Cartland too has turned to a major photographic supplier - Marion & Co. But he has not settled for one of their popular stock designs, and every element is directly related to him or his studio. In choosing a picture of Windsor Castle he is identifying with the town in which he works and defining himself as a member of its community. In the lower illustration he is presenting himself as a photographer whose skills and achievements are recognised by his peers. This illustration shows the obverse and reverse of two medals, dated 1886 and 1887, from exhibitions of the Photographic Society (of London) - the organisation that was founded in 1853 and that later became the Royal Photographic Society. These medals prompt further investigation and lead, via sources described in the 'Exhibitions' chapter, to more information about the photographer. A member of the society, Cartland won his medals for a picture of dogs photographed for the Queen (in 1886) and a picture of elephants involved in the Golden Jubilee celebrations at Windsor (in 1887). The elephant photograph was taken at 8 o'clock in the evening. Cartland also submitted non-winning pictures in 1887 and 1892, including an image grandly entitled 'She thinks of Napoli o'er the Ocean'. It will be noticed that Cartland makes no boast of the royal patronage of which the dog picture is evidence. The associations of a royal castle and the portrait of the late Prince Albert on the medals may, nevertheless, have an unconscious effect. The powers of suggestion may also be at work in the representation of the medals, for showing both sides of each could help the casual observer to assume that more medals are depicted than is really the case.

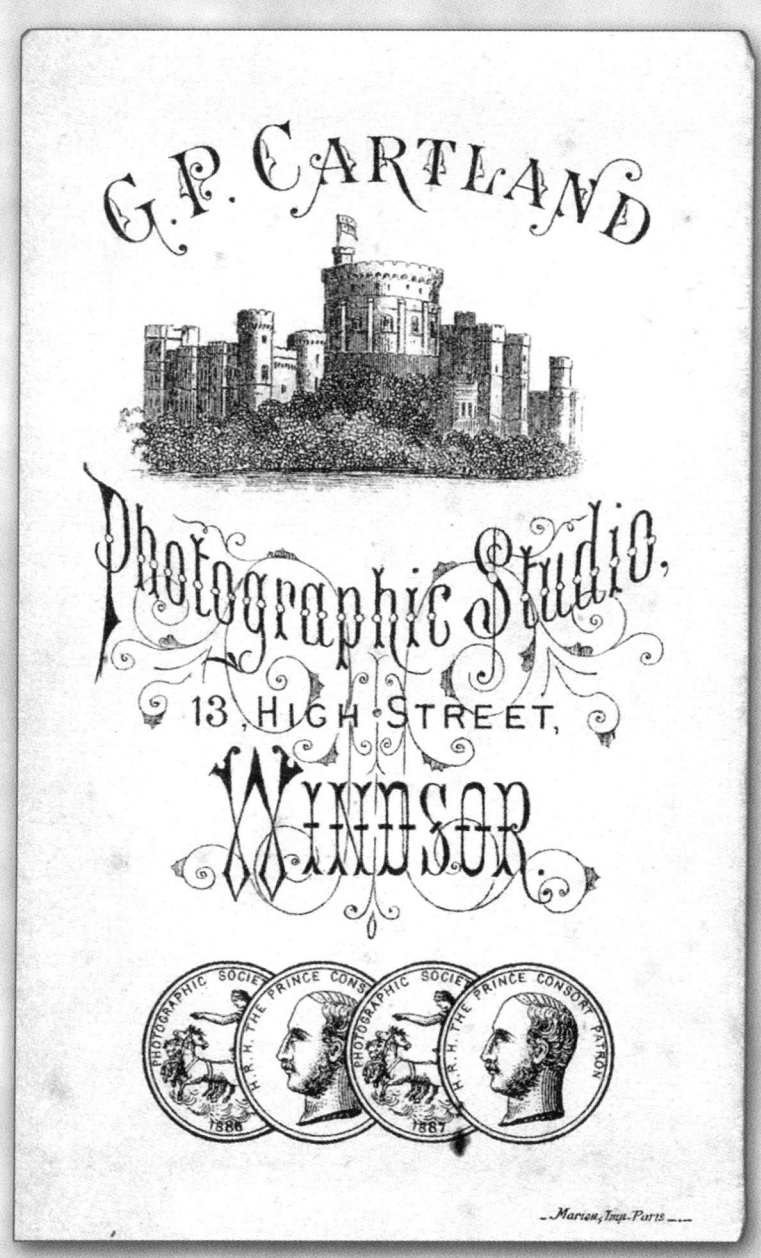

Figure 6

3. The images

Whilst it's fairly safe to assume that a studio's mounts all reflect decisions made by the principal of the business, the same cannot be said of all its images. It would be naïve to imagine that every photograph is the sole product of the person in whose name the operation is conducted. Some pictures may have been taken by assistants, and processing and finishing may have been assigned to one or more employees. Not for the first time, Jasper Wright of King's Lynn provides a useful illustration. In 1898 he employed James Speight as his assistant to accompany him on assignments outside the studio and to take some responsibility for the smaller branches in Swaffham, Hunstanton and Fakenham. He already had a Miss Porter and a Miss Hammond as assistants, though their duties are not clear, and a Mr Turner was working as a retoucher. In addition, Lewis Reeve seems to have been serving his time as an apprentice. So it is often difficult to be sure that a picture has been taken by the photographer whose name it bears. In practice, the smaller the business, the more likely a picture is to be the principal's own work, and where there were satellite studios, they were more likely to be managed by an employee. Some photographers, however, made a point of reassuring the public that all pictures were taken under their personal supervision, and the fact remains that all pictures from a photographer's studio reflect the standards and practice of his business, as well as show the backgrounds and furnishings in which he has invested. It follows that, though we must be cautious in the assertions that we make, we can use a studio's products as evidence that sheds some light on a photographer's working life.

Assessing an early photographer's outdoor pictures is not so very different from assessing those of his more modern equivalent. Framing and composition can be considered, as can the way the eye is led from one part of the image to another. The sharpness of focus can be examined, and the relationships between foreground and background, mass and detail can be weighed up. It's necessary to remember, though, that exposure times were longer and that lighting was potentially a problem. It could be difficult to reproduce small surface differences within darker areas (especially since the end result would be in monochrome), and pale areas could easily become burnt out. The sky, in particular, set a challenge: the length of exposure needed to model trees, rocks or buildings was often more than required for skies, which tended therefore to appear uniformly white or pale grey. (One way of solving the problem was to make separate exposures for land and sky and then combine two negatives on the final print.) If an early photographer seems able to overcome such difficulties, his skills deserve some respect. If, however, his skies are expanses of undifferentiated pallor, he should not be too severely criticised.

But it's when the attention focuses on studio portraits that an informed understanding of the early photographer's task is especially useful. There were fashions in studio backgrounds and furnishings, and there were conventions concerning how men and women should appear. The factors a researcher might need to consider are numerous, and since they vary from picture to picture, they are not entirely predictable. There are, though, some obvious topics to explore, and they resolve themselves into a series of questions one can ask oneself (though not every question will be appropriate for every picture).

First, there are technical concerns to think about.

How has the lighting been handled? We can't see what arrangement of windows and skylights the studio has, or what blinds or reflectors have been used to manipulate the light, but we can see whether the light is even or directional, whether the features are clearly defined, whether shirts are bleached out, or whether the folds of dark dresses are distinct. Once electricity arrived in studios, new kinds of artifice became possible and can sometimes be discerned. The illumination might, for instance, have been organised to correspond with the direction of the painted lighting effects on a backcloth.

Is there a good depth of focus? Are hands and faces defined with equal clarity, and is fabric as sharp as features? The earlier cameras had their limitations, which a good photographer would seek to minimise. He could ensure that hands and faces were in the same plane and thus at the same distance from the camera. (In addition, he thereby ensured that the hands would not appear disproportionately large.) Alternatively, he could choose to concentrate on the face, ensuring that any imperfection affected only the less important details of the picture.

Did he switch from albumen paper to carbon printing, and if so, at what stage? Carbon processes offered darker, richer tones, but many professionals were in no great hurry to make the change. The white highlights of carbon paper and the creamy or yellowish highlights of albumen papers make it possible to distinguish between them. Carbon printing also offered greater permanence than the albumen printing of the 1880s and 1890s. Albumen prints of the 1860s have proved less susceptible to fading, however, because more chloride was generally used in the preparation of the paper. A faded albumen image from the later years of the century is, therefore, a victim of recipes of its time. It should not be taken as evidence of poor printing or fixing by the individual photographer.

What standards of finishing were usual in his studio? Care, or lack of it, may be seen in the trimming of prints and the fixing of the picture to its mount. Finishing was often the work of employees, but the end results went out under the principal's name and therefore reflect on him. Occasionally a fingerprint or thumbprint can be seen in the corner of an image. This may have been acquired during the application of wet collodion to the photographic plate rather than at the printing stage. Since the preparation of wet plates was a critical stage in the process, it was often - in smaller businesses at least - undertaken by the photographer himself. (For family historians in such instances, the charge of carelessness is to a degree offset by the possibility of owning an ancestral thumbprint.)

The studio and its contents also deserve attention.

What range of backdrops did he use over the years? Is there evidence of varied settings? Use of only a few backdrops is not necessarily a sign of a practitioner of limited resources or ambitions. It may be a matter of preference. At Elliott & Fry's Baker Street studio, by the early 1880s, there were 26 backdrops in one of their operating rooms. But James Russell of Worthing, as a matter of policy, used very few backcloths and favoured a simple setting.

What can be said about the quality of backcloths? Many of them appear distinctly impressive, but amateurish backgrounds are occasionally in evidence, especially in the early years of the twentieth century. It's also worth considering whether any backcloths appear to have been painted specifically for the studio in which they appear. Many photographers bought their supplies from major suppliers, among which L W Seavey of New York and Engelmann & Schneider of Dresden were particularly prominent. Others commissioned the work locally or even undertook the painting themselves, and this is occasionally evident in the depiction of local detail. Many studios - some of them inland - had a coastal scene in their selection, for example. But Alfred Read of Great Yarmouth had one with a fishing boat bearing the letters YH (the port's registration code), which made the background specific to the location.

What range of furniture and accessories can be seen in his photographs, and how did he make use of them? Dating pictures can help towards deciding whether a photographer kept up with current furnishing trends. It can allow, too, the comparison of images from the same period of time. This gives the researcher the chance to notice whether the same props and furniture were used for most sitters, or whether changes were made to suit the subject. The surroundings set up for a man were sometimes different from those contrived for a woman. The solidity of any background furniture can also be worth checking. Genuine chairs were needed for sitting on and genuine tables for leaning, but other items, such as bookcases, might be painted rather than three-dimensional. Furniture that is real without needing to be suggests substantiality in more ways than one.

Is there any use of 'architectural' furniture? If so, is there evidence of its adaptability? False pillars, plinths, walls and balustrades were popular studio accessories. Though solid enough to lean on, they were not constructed of stone, for they had to be moved in and out of position. Sometimes, when a series of photographs has survived, it is possible to see how such items have been adapted to the subject. A plinth, for example, could be made in sections. This not only made it easy to carry; it also allowed a section to be added or removed according to the height of the person about to rest an elbow on the structure.

Is there any sign of a posing stand being used? Until the 1860s, and sometimes much later, photographers used a headrest or neck-clamp to help the sitter remain still throughout the several-second exposure. The base of such a device can sometimes be seen behind a male subject's feet, though many photographers sought to hide it by pulling across the lower part of a curtain and draping it around the bottom of the stand. (Such subterfuge was not necessary for female subjects, whose voluminous skirts hid any evidence of posing aids.) I used to assume that a visible posing stand was evidence of carelessness on the photographer's part, but I have become less certain. A glimpse of a stand is not very usual, but nor is it a rarity. I begin to suspect that some photographers scorned the artifice of clumsily angled curtains, knew their purpose was obvious, and chose to dispense with pretence.

The way in which a photographer posed his subjects is of interest in its own right.

How does he suggest suitable qualities in the sitter? The aim may be to suggest one or more of a range of virtues: authority, gravity, modesty, pensiveness and so on. Consider both the desired effect and how stance, seated position, angle of head, accessories and direction of gaze contribute to it. If, to the twenty-first century eye, an element of gender stereotyping is present, that would have been acceptable - even desirable - during the nineteenth century (and for much of the twentieth).

Has he encouraged a natural expression? Has he helped the subject overcome the stiffness that could be produced by long exposures, neck-clamps, unfamiliar surroundings, Sunday-best clothes and the disturbing novelty of the experience? The Victorians were not generally interested in smiling for the camera. The photographer's task was to capture the client's dignity and respectability, not to present him or her as cheerfully inconsequential. But that did not mean that a glowering grimness was necessary. In writing about portraiture, photographers often expressed a desire to capture a 'pleasing expression', and the best of them managed to record a thoughtful or intelligent seriousness rather than a wooden impassivity.

What does he do about hands? When observed, people are often unsure of what to do with their hands. But a photographer should be able to overcome that awkwardness.

How does he manage children? Do they appear over-awed by the occasion? Is any particular technique used to help them keep steady or to engage their interest? Many photographers provided some props or novelty items to keep children occupied, but it's often hard to judge whether a toy belongs to the studio or was brought along by the sitter.

How does he handle groups? Groups present organisational problems: people of different heights may have to be accommodated; vertical and horizontal arrangement must both be considered if people are to be fitted into a rectangular frame of conventional proportions; and it will often be necessary to compose the picture in way that indicates seniority within the group. The question of seniority or dominance will often apply even in the smallest of groups - the portrait of two people. It is therefore worth observing how the photographer poses the participants in a way that reflects their relationship.

Has he created a subtext? It will be evident from what has already been said, that the job of the photographer was often to suggest the qualities of his subjects and the nature of the relationships between them. There may be other underlying messages, too - in the careful display of a ring, say, or in the presence of a photograph in the background.

What decisions has the photographer made? This is the question that encompasses all the others. The sitter may, of course, have expressed concerns or preferences. This will be especially true in the case of intentionally commemorative pictures that record engagements, bereavements and childhood rites of passage. But the pose has still largely, if not entirely, been directed by the photographer. That direction could take different forms. Some practitioners fiercely advocated that the sitter should be verbally directed but never touched. Others ignored this dictum. Camille Silvy was apparently one of those who preferred a hands-on approach, since he put on a fresh pair of white gloves as each new client entered the portrait room. But however the guidance was delivered, each portrait shows, in such matters as the angle of the head and the deployment of hands, decisions made by the professional.

As with mounts, a mere handful of examples can be examined to show what can be learned from the images themselves. It should be added that these are single examples. It is hoped that researchers will have a greater range of photographs to explore, and that will help them towards a more balanced understanding of how a photographer went about his business.

Figure 7 shows a carte de visite from the 1860s by S Wiseman of Southampton. The studio setting is fairly simple, as was usual at the time. But the furniture is solid enough to take a little weight and it has a nicely turned leg; the dado is applied rather than merely painted on; and there's a richness to the floor covering's pattern. The result is a suitably dignified setting for a man of substance. The subject has been given something to do with his hands: one rests comfortably on the table, and the other holds his pince-nez as if about to lift it to scrutinise and deliver judgement. The left arm is extended confidently away from the body and the feet are planted firmly but a little apart (incidentally demonstrating that no posing stand has been found necessary). The man's eyes are focussed on something or somebody to the right of the camera and his facial expression is alert. He could be about to speak. In short, the photographer has created a subtext that establishes the subject as a man of affairs: he is assured, decisive, and a person to be taken seriously. The photograph has good tonal gradation, with a range of shades in the dark clothes that is especially evident in the subject's left sleeve. The features are quite well defined, too, though the exposure needed for the fabrics has been a little too much for the side-whiskers, the hairline and the right hand.

Also from the 1860s is **Figure 8**, a carte de visite by James Saunders of Lowestoft. Here, too, the studio setting is simple, but Saunders has also invested in one of the backcloths that became popular as the decade progressed, and a little of it can be seen behind the curtain at the edge of the picture. The composition is very effective. The two young women - presumably sisters - have been placed at different levels and facing in opposite directions, as if they inhabit separate but contiguous worlds. Though neither looks at the other, they are linked partly by the hand of one sister on the chair back of the other, and partly by the triangular shape that they form. (Triangular composition was frequently advocated, and crinolines made it easily achievable, but it did not always take such dramatic form.) The women's body language is very different from that of the man in Figure 7. Arms are kept close to the body, heads are slightly bowed and eyes are directed well away from the camera. The accepted female persona was demure and unassertive, and the photographer has captured these qualities. The conventional choice of prop for the seated sister reinforces the effect. As well as occupying her hands, the book suggests an appropriate thoughtfulness. Indeed, it is not fully closed, as if she has broken off reading for the sake of the portrait, keeping a thumb between the pages so that she can quickly resume. Both faces are well illuminated, though more light falls on the seated figure and rather washes out the pattern on the front of her skirt. One might wish the picture to be more tightly cropped to cut out the top of the wall and the glimpse of irrelevant backcloth. But the picture is still striking. Problems with depth of focus mean that the sister nearer to the lens is less sharply defined, but that is perhaps a price worth paying for the overall effect.

Figure 7

Figure 8

Figure 9

A carte de visite by C Banyard serves as **Figure 9**. (No address is given on the mount, and there were photographers in both Norfolk and Suffolk with this name.) The picture probably dates from the early 1870s, and it takes us into a less assured studio environment than the two previous examples. The setting is redolent of the 1860s, but the impression is less of elegant simplicity than of tackiness and clutter. The dado is real enough, and Banyard has used a painted backcloth, but its edge can be seen to be a few inches in front of the back wall, which undermines any sense of illusion. The curtain is painted and lacks the sense of weight that accompanies the fabric in Wiseman's and Saunders' studios. Failure to crop out the top of the wall is much more disturbing than in Figure 8; part of a large frame intrudes into the picture at the bottom left; and a curious desk, with stuck-on ornamentation and incongruously spartan drawers, is turned sideways on so that the construction layers of its back panel are displayed. Verticals are not quite vertical, and horizontals are not quite horizontal. It isn't surprising that the man seems uncomfortably posed. The base of a headrest is visible. One foot is placed slightly ahead of the other, as if he were about to step forward (though, if he did, his right foot would catch the bottom of the desk). The cane is slightly at an angle, and a jauntily angled cane was recommended as one way of achieving a triangular composition. But it is perhaps not jaunty enough, serving only to add to the miscellany of near-verticals. The face has the frozen stare of which Victorian photographs are often accused. Such criticisms often derive from a failure to understand what our ancestors required of their portraits, but on this occasion the charge seems reasonable. We are not looking at the work of a man who has taken naturally to his occupation.

Figure 10 is a carte de visite from the Ambleside studio of J Bowness, and it brings us back into the realms of professional competence. The costume and the back of the mount indicate a date in the 1870s, but the setting seems advanced for its time. The emphasis on the texture of bark and foliage is more commonly seen in studios of the 1880s. Planed wood and rather restrained nature were more usual in the 1870s. So Bowness' setting, though not unique, puts him in the vanguard of taste. He also uses the setting well. The young woman is seen in the countryside rather than simply in front of it, and care has been taken to disguise the point where plain background meets studio floor. A slightly jarring interface between studio carpet and painted sylvan background was by no means unusual. It seems to have been the occasion for a willing suspension of disbelief. The arrangement of this setting is therefore a mark of Bowness' thoughtfulness. Lighting presents no problems: face, hands and clothes are all well defined. There is some loss of sharpness towards the edge of the picture, as can be seen in the foliage at the bottom corners, but this arose from lens limitations. What was important was to make sure that key details were in focus, and that has been achieved. The pose looks comfortable; the facial expression is agreeable whilst stopping just short of a smile; and the branches

Figure 10

provide natural resting places for the hands. The subject's body is at a slightly different angle from her face, which points directly at the camera. But, as befits maidenly charms, her eyes do not quite meet the gaze of the lens.

George Washington Wilson's Aberdeen studio is the source of the carte de visite shown as **Figure 11**. It was taken in the 1870s, some time after Wilson was awarded a Royal Warrant in 1873, and it shows the photographer posing a group of subjects with very disparate heights. He opts for the popular triangular composition and organises his subjects on three levels - standing on the floor, sitting on the chair, and sitting on the back of the chair. The off-centre apex of the triangle is balanced by the curtain and the left-hand girl. The two siblings who are closest in height are used to contain the ensemble. The child perched on the back of the chair is securely held by her father (whose other hand rests protectively on another daughter's shoulder), and further reassurance is derived from resting a hand on her sister's head. The girls in the darker dresses have been invited to bring forefingers and thumbs together, so that their hands are neither stiffly open nor tightly clenched. The hands of the fourth girl are occupied by an illustrated magazine, which is open at pictures of Punch and Judy. She might have brought this to the studio with her, but it could have come from the studio's store of props. The general air of solemnity is appropriate for a Victorian studio, but there may be an element of tension in the girls' expressions which the mother's absence could go a long way towards explaining. The picture's subtext, supported by the grouping, concerns the father as protector and provider, and it's altogether possible that his wife's death has made him the sole protector. The limitations of the camera's lens are very evident in the lower part of the picture, but the photographer has made sure that all the faces are in focus. There is, however, a jarring note in the presence of superfluous furniture. One chair is used to accommodate two of the subjects, and one footstool (which she no longer needs) has been used to help a child onto the seat. An extra stool is tucked under the chair, and part of a further chair or chaise is visible to our right. This gives the picture a total - seen and implied - of twenty-six feet. This seems rather excessive and perhaps lessens the impact of a thoughtfully composed and poignant picture.

Figure 12 shows children more at their ease. It is a carte de visite from the Brighton School of Photography. The business also had a branch in Bath, and both Mr and Mrs Charles Hawkins were involved in the operation. Studio dating suggests the picture was taken in the late 1880s, which is rather late for the use of posing stands, the bases of which can be seen behind both boys. But anything that helped children keep still was doubtless worth considering. On this occasion, at any rate, the stands have been used effectively, and the brothers show no sign of discomfort at their presence. In fact, the leaning angles of their upper bodies suggest a nonchalant ease. One hand of each boy holds the brim of a boater, and the unoccupied hands hang

Figure 11

Figure 12

very naturally from supported forearms. The brothers look just to the left of the camera, and it's possible that the photographer has placed (or is holding) something there to engage their attention. But whatever aids have been used, the photographer has succeeded in encouraging an easy composure and has helped the boys feel like confident young men, even though they have not yet graduated into long trousers. The studio furniture is reassuringly substantial, with an ornately carved desk and a well-padded fringed chair that entered the studio in the 1870s. A footrest has been used to allow the seated boy to adopt a more comfortable position. The photograph has been printed on albumen paper, though this will not be particularly evident in black-and-white reproduction. The use of albumen paper in the late 1880s was not unusual, but nor was it the only option. It should therefore be seen as a matter of choice by a photographer who would rather stay with softer warmer tones than switch to the more dramatic intensity offered by carbon printing processes.

The postcard used for **Figure 13** is credited to J H Jamieson, of Preston and Wrexham, and was taken in the years just before the First World War. Jamieson appears to have set up in business in the early years of the century, and his studio certainly bears the stamp of the new era. Gone is the furniture with plush upholstery, and gone is the dark turned or carved wood. Instead we see the stylishly pale and clean-cut look of a seat that's influenced by Scottish art nouveau design. The backcloth, too, reflects the taste of the new century, with its depiction of a recessed leaded window in a wood-panelled wall. Some early twentieth century backcloths combined novelty of painted location with some crudeness of execution, but Jamieson has used a background that represents the higher end of the market. It shows a quietly impressive interior, and it pays some attention to directional lighting effects, with light coming through the window, catching the ledge and the curtain, and casting the shadow of the mullion on the sill. The photographer has then picked up the backcloth's messages in the management of his own lighting. The young woman appears backlit, as if through the window. This throws the front of her skirt and parts of the seat into deep shadow. But enough supplementary (or reflected) lighting has been used to reduce and soften the shadows on her face. As a result, the sense of directional lighting is preserved, the features are not lost, and a sense of unity between setting and subject is achieved. Notice, too, a weakening of gender stereotyping. The woman is, of course, still modest and composed. But the closeness of arms to body has gone, and the assurance in the placing of hands is more reminiscent of the man in Figure 7 than the women in Figure 8. The body leans slightly forward, as if ready to respond or act; the tilt of the head seems almost questioning; and the eyes meet those of the viewer without reserve or diffidence. The subject may be the New Woman (and she is certainly wearing one of the V-necked blouses - with modesty insert - that some commentators found so forward), but the photographer has helped her find a way of expressing her confidence on camera.

Figure 13

Figure 14

A cabinet print by Henry Peach Robinson serves as **Figure 14**, and it takes us back to the 1870s for a final reflection on what makes a good photograph. Recognised in his time and now as a serious photographic artist, Robinson was a professional of considerable stature who ran portrait studios for over thirty years. By the time this picture was taken, he had won at least forty medals at photographic exhibitions across Europe and in the USA. He served for many years on the Council of what was to become the Royal Photographic Society; he was a founder member of the group of artist photographers known as The Linked Ring; and he wrote several books on studio techniques and practice. An example of work from his studio seems more likely than most to offer an understanding of what constituted skilful professional practice.

The picture shows a married couple looking at a book. The setting could hardly be simpler. The husband sits in a chair, little of which can be seen, at a small table that's covered by a heavy, richly-patterned cloth. That is all. The floor is out of shot and the background is absolutely plain. Robinson certainly had some backcloths. He scorned to buy them ready-made from the likes of Seavey and preferred to paint his own. But in this photograph there is nothing to distract us from the couple and what they are doing. The composition is based on the ever-reliable triangle, within which a clearly discernable curved line leads from the woman's head, down her arm and along the man's arm to the book he is reading. But there is also an invisible line created by the eyes: her glance leads us to his head, from where his glance leads to the book. The focus is sharp and clothes and features are both well lit. Highlights on her cheek and his forehead are kept within control, and his pale trousers, which could very easily have been overexposed, have some differentiation of light and shade. Their pallid expanse has, incidentally, been slightly reduced by having the frock of his coat lap over the upper part of his right leg. As a whole, the lighting is gentle, and a range of surfaces and textures is captured without the need for tonal extremes. The man sits slightly turned towards the camera, but his wife is kept sideways on so that the details of her skirt can be shown to advantage. The subjects, predictably, conform to stereotype. The husband sits while his wife stands. He is occupied with important matters in his book. She is in attendance on him, perhaps gazing at him as much as at the pages. Her wedding and engagement rings are clearly visible as her hand rests lightly on his arm. But stereotyping is something to be observed rather than complained of. It showed our ancestors to themselves as they wished to be seen, and though the underlying assumptions about the husband/wife relationship may not be entirely to twenty-first century taste, it would be foolish of us to blame yesterday for failing to be today. It should, in addition, be admitted that the couple have been encouraged to play out their roles in a way that suggests tenderness and affection, without undermining the values of dignity and respectability. The photographer has used his experience to create a unified and harmonious image.

A sense of perspective

An afterthought seems appropriate. Sometimes a study of his images will reveal what is special about a photographer, showing ways in which he differed from the mass of his fellows. In many more cases, when the available pictures have been scrutinised, a photographer will prove to have been unremarkable. He will have been observed at work, doing the things most photographers did in the way most photographers did them, displaying the conventional taste and deploying the customary skills of his time. But the effort taken to understand that taste and recognise those skills is not wasted. It leads, rather, to an insight into the way he learned the lessons of his occupation and put them to use, and no apology is needed for an honest but undistinguished career. Genealogy is not only for those with a line stretching back to the Norman Conquest. In much the same way, a photographic ancestor does not have to be a luminary like Robinson in order to be interesting.

CHAPTER ELEVEN
Additional websites

Many websites have already been mentioned, and some of these are worth further exploration for their coverage of history, studio background, formats and processes. It is assumed that researchers will generally discover such possibilities for themselves. A select few are featured again here in a new context, but the main concern is to draw attention to some additional sites that deal with aspects of early photography, but that have not been included in the lists given so far. I have tried to organise them thematically, though some individual sites have broader interests than the themes by which they are listed.

Early photography and photographic history

City Gallery
www.city-gallery.com
The site was founded in 1995 by Steve Noblock. Much of its content is specifically USA-related, but there is plenty of information on history and formats in its 'Learning' section.

History of photography
www.rleggat.com/photohistory
Robert Leggat's site deals with photography from its beginnings until the 1920s. Its treatment of individual photographers has already been

mentioned as a multi-studio biographical source, but its extensive coverage of processes, styles and movements should also be noticed.

International Museum of Photography and Film
www.eastmanhouse.org
The site has a number of online collections, a few of which are by British photographers, but it is also a good starting point for learning about George Eastman's innovations and the Kodak revolution.

'Ireland's earliest photographer ...'
http://arts.jrank.org/pages/10781/Ireland's.html
Useful as an introduction to early photography in Ireland, including Northern Ireland.

Midley history of early photography
www.midley.co.uk
The site is home to a collection of academic articles by R Derek Wood on photographic history, the daguerreotype and the diorama. It was due to go offline in July 2010, but it could still be found at the above address in the early part of 2011. When the address ceases to work, it should be possible to find the site's contents at www.webarchive.org.uk/wayback/archive/20100311230213/http://www.midley.co.uk

Nineteenth-century photography
www.ajmorris.com/roots/photo/index.php
Part of the website of Andrew J Morris, this is concerned with history, processes and dating. There is a strong North American perspective.

Wonderful world of early photography
www.neatorama.com/2006/08/29/the-wonderful-world-of-early-photography
A variety of aspects of early photography are looked at in a manner that is perhaps lightweight, but the site is well illustrated and entertaining.

Early processes and formats

About.com: Inventors
http://inventors.about.com/od/pstartinventions/a/stilphotography.htm
A useful site for information about a number of innovations.

Ambrotype.co.uk
http://ambrotype.co.uk
A brief introduction to the process.

Art of the photogravure
www.photogravure.com/resources/glossary.html
The site features articles and notes relating to a range of processes.

Daguerrian Society
http://daguerre.org/index.php
There is a distinct US focus, but the 'Resources' section of the website has a great deal of information about the daguerreotype process and about early studios and practice. One page (http://daguerre.org/society/annual/toc.html) has an index to the society's Daguerreian Annual, copies of which can be bought (at a premium price) by non-members.

Frederick Scott Archer 1813-1857
www.samackenna.co.uk/fsa/FSArcher.html
Set up to celebrate the inventor of wet collodion photography, Seán MacKenna's site includes Archer's own account of his process.

Jack & Beverly's photographic collectables
http://brightbytes.com/collection/photo.html
Sections on cased images and stereo photography are included.

Nicéphore Niépce House
www.niepce.com/home-us.html
Niépce might be described as the pre-inventor of photography. Daguerre collaborated with him for some years, and his own success owed a significant debt to Niépce's pioneering work. The site focuses on the earliest period of photographic experiment.

PhotoHistory
www.photographyhistory.net/complete-index
This page is part of a wider-ranging site and provides links to a series of essays and articles written by early photographers.

Scully and Osterman Studio
www.collodion.org
The site offers a fund of information on early processes (including the modern use of them) and focuses particularly on collodion photography and salt paper printing.

Tintype.co.uk
http://tintype.co.uk
A brief introduction to the process.

Photographic equipment and suppliers

Antique & 19th Century Cameras
www.antiquewoodcameras.com
The title of Rob Niederman's site is self-explanatory. A carte de visite camera can be found at www.antiquewoodcameras.com/wetpl1.htm.

Early photography
www.earlyphotography.co.uk/index.html
An extensive collection of cameras and photographic equipment from the 1850s to the 1950s is illustrated and described. Additional information is given about manufacturers and patents.

Luminous Lint
www.luminous-lint.com/app/home/H1
Alan Griffiths' site repays systematic exploration. Suppliers, studio backcloths, dark tents and photographic wagons are just a few of the topics touched on.

Michael Pritchard – Photographic history
www.mpritchard.com/photographic_history.php
This page of Michael Pritchard's website reflects his interest in photographic manufacturers and retailers. It displays some illustrations of premises, but his research extends much further than the site can show, and he is willing to answer questions.

Museum of Science and Industry
www.mosi.org.uk/collections/about-the-collections/information-sheets/people-information-sheets
The pages on individual photographers have already been mentioned, but there are also pages on some photographic inventors and suppliers.

Marginal sources for biographical and career information

Pre-Raphaelite photographers
www.libfl.ru/pre-raph/index.html
Most of the photographers mentioned are amateurs, but a few very well-known professionals are included.

Victorian Web
www.victorianweb.org/photos/index.html
This page leads to examples of portraits by a number of eminent photographers, but the site's primary interest is in the sitters.

Tangential topics

(This category covers sites that are only partly relevant and sites that deal with aspects of professional photography that fall largely outside this book's timescale or other terms of reference.)

Books online
www.archive.org | http://books.google.co.uk | http://openlibrary.org
A number of websites specialise in making digitised copies of old and rare books available (wholly or in part) online. Some early photographic texts are to be found on such sites, three of which are listed above.

Ilford Limited
www.greatyarmouthphotographic.co.uk/ilfordltd
Paul Godfrey's Ilford site is devoted to the photo processing and finishing business that became increasingly important to photographers after the First World war.

Photo Detective
www.photodetective.co.uk/Index.html
Geoff Caulton's main concern is with the dating of twentieth-century photographs, but there is also some useful mention of studio chains and photographic formats.

Photographic libraries
www.photographiclibraries.com
Helpful to researchers seeking to identify archives and collections beyond the UK.

Seaside photographer
www.greatyarmouthphotographic.co.uk/seasidephotographer
This is another Paul Godfrey site, which focuses on the East Norfolk and Suffolk coastal areas, and which includes a look at the walking pictures of the 1920s and later.

Walking Pictures
http://gohomeonapostcard.wordpress.com
The site currently has a strong focus on the promenade trade in Bridlington and Margate, but its geographical coverage should widen in time.

The care of photographs

(A number of sites offering advice on the preservation and care of photographs can be found on the web. This is a selection.)

Benson Ford Research Center
www.thehenryford.org/research/caring/prints.aspx

Library of Congress
www.loc.gov/preserv/care/photo.html

National Archives
www.archives.gov/preservation/family-archives/index.html

Photographic Materials Group of the American Institute for the Conservation of Historic and Artistic Works
http://cool.conservation-us.org/coolaic/sg/pmg/caringforphotos.html

Links, blogs and discussions

British photographic history
http://britishphotohistory.ning.com
Founded by Michael Pritchard in 2009, this site occupies the ground where blog and forum meet. Only members may contribute, and the membership list is studded with the names of eminent photographic historians. But anyone can follow the informed and often absorbing discussions. The site also keeps its followers up-to-date with news of exhibitions and events.

Cyndi's list
www.cyndislist.com/photos.htm#Photographers
The photography page of Cyndi Howell's list provides links to many of the sites mentioned in this book, but it is likely to be updated much more frequently. It also has links to many sites that fall outside this book's terms of reference, including some directories of overseas photographers. There is, in addition, a useful bibliography.

Family photos
http://blog.findmypast.co.uk/category/family-photos
This is part of the Findmypast website, where Jayne Shrimpton discusses various aspects of old photographs. The emphasis is on dating and interpretation.

Family Tree Forum
www.familytreeforum.com/content.php/326-Victorian-and-EdwardianPhotographers
Many of the links on this page are to sites already mentioned, but there are a number of links to sources for overseas photographers, and they are not always the same sources as appear on Cyndi's List (above).

Jacolette
http://jacolette.wordpress.com/about
The primary concern of this blog is Irish snapshot and vernacular photography, but there is some reference to studio professionals.

Photo-Sleuth
http://photo-sleuth.blogspot.com
Brett Payne's blog offers comment on a wide range of topics relating to early photography and studio photographers.

Roger Vaughan picture library - keyword search
www.cartes.freeuk.com/fusion.htm
This serves as a link page to the numerous websites of photographic historian Roger Vaughan. It also provides a search facility for seven of them.

Watch the birdie - The world of the Victorian photographer
http://qvictoria.wordpress.com
Christine Hibbert's blog touches on various aspects of early photography, including mounts and women photographers, and her desire to help correspondents is very evident. The site includes a number of photographer lists that fall short of being directories and should be regarded as work in progress.

CHAPTER TWELVE
General bibliography

Printed works that may give useful information on individual photographers have been already been listed, and they are not, for the most part, repeated here. An exception has been made in a very few cases, where the potential value of a book goes well beyond the context in which it was previously mentioned. Otherwise, this bibliography aims to indicate more general background reading for the student of early photography and, in particular, to suggest material relevant to the chapters headed 'The photographic context' and 'The photographs themselves'. Organisation is thematic, though works are not always wholly devoted to one theme, and some could qualify for inclusion in more than one category.

General reference works

Hannavy, John (ed.), *Encyclopedia of nineteenth century photography* (Abingdon: Routledge, 2005).

Lenman, Robin (ed.), *The Oxford companion to the photograph* (Oxford: Oxford University Press, 2005).

The study of photographers and photography

Johnson, William S, *Nineteenth century photography: an annotated bibliography* (Boston: G K Hall, 1990).
Palmquist, Peter E (ed.), *Photographers, a sourcebook for historical research, featuring Richard Rudisill's completely revised Directories of photographers* (Nevada City: Carl Mautz, 2000).
Roosens, Laurent & Salu, Luc, *History of photography: a bibliography of books*, two volumes (London: Mansell, 1989, 1994).
Sennett, Robert S, *Photography and photographers to 1900: an annotated bibliography* (New York: Garland Publishing, 1985).
Stevenson, Sara & Morrison-Low, Alison, *Scottish photography - a bibliography: 1839-1989* (Edinburgh: Salvia Books, 1990).

History of photography

Burnett-Brown, Anthony, Gray, Michael & Roberts, Russell, *Specimens and marvels: William Henry Fox Talbot and the invention of photography* (New York, Aperture Foundation, 2000).
Coe, Brian, *The birth of photography: the story of the formative years 1800-1900* (London: Ash & Grant, 1976).
Daniels, Patrick, *Early photography* (London: Academy Editions, 1978).
Gernsheim, Helmut, *The origins of photography* (London: Thames & Hudson, 1982).
Gernsheim, Helmut, *The rise of photography 1850-1880: the collodion age* (London: Thames & Hudson, 1988).
Gernsheim, Helmut & Alison, *A concise history of photography* (London: Thames & Hudson, 1971).
Harker, Margaret, *Victorian and Edwardian photographs* (London: Letts, 1975) [SoG shelf mark: TB/POR 9].
Macdonald, Gus, Camera: *Victorian eyewitness* (London: Batsford, 1979).

The professional photographer and his studio

Baden, Pritchard H, *The Photographic studios of Europe* (London: Piper & Carter, 1882. OCR edition - LaVergne: Kessinger Publishing, 2010) .
Briggs, Asa & Miles, Archie, *A Victorian portrait: Victorian life and values as seen through the work of studio photographers* (London: Harper & Row, 1989) [SoG shelf mark: PR/PHO].
Hannavy, John, *The Victorian professional photographer* (Princes Risborough: Shire, 1980).

Hannavy, John, *Victorian photographers at work* (Princes Risborough: Shire, 1997) [SoG shelf mark: PR/PHO].

Heyert, Elisabeth, *The glass-house years: Victorian portrait photography 1839-1870* (London: George Prior, 1979).

Lee, David, *The Victorian Studio 1* in *British Journal of Photography* (London: Henry Greenwood & Co, 7 February 1986).

Lee, David, *The Victorian Studio 2* in *British Journal of Photography* (London: Henry Greenwood & Co, 14 February 1986).

Linkman, Audrey, *The itinerant photographer in Britain, 1850-1880* in *History of Photography*, volume 14 (London: Taylor & Francis, January-March 1990).

Linkman, Audrey, *The Victorians: photographic portraits* (London: Tauris Parke, 1993).

Pols, Robert, *Understanding old photographs* (Witney: Robert Boyd, 1995).

Early techniques and processes

Baxter, William Raleigh, *Photography, including the daguerreotype, calotype, chrysotype, etc.; familiarly explained, being a treatise on its objects and uses* (London: Henry Renshaw, 1842. OCR edition - LaVergne: Kessinger Publishing, 2008).

Coe, Brian & Haworth-Booth, Mark, *A guide to early photographic processes* (London: Victoria & Albert Museum, 1983).

Estabrooke, Edward M, *The ferrotype and how to make it* (New York: Morgan & Morgan, first edition 1872. Reprinted - London: Fountain Press, 1972).

Forbes, Heather (ed.), *Beautiful ambrotypes* (London: Travelling Light, 1989).

Gernsheim, Helmut & Alison, *L J M Daguerre: the history of the diorama and the daguerreotype* (New York: Dover, 1978).

Hawkes, Henry Philip, *Photography in a nutshell* (London: Iliffe and Sons, first edition 1891. OCR edition (1898 version) - LaVergne: Kessinger Publishing, 2008. CD facsimile of 1899 version - Cinderford: Archive CD Books, 2006) [SoG shelf mark: CD-ROM cabinet : PR/PHO].

Lea, Matthew Carey, *A manual of photography: intended as a text book for beginners and a book of reference for advanced photographers* (Philadelphia: Benerman & Wilson, 1868. Reprinted - Michigan: University of Michigan Library, 2006).

Linkman, Audrey, *Cheap tin trade: the ferrotype portrait in Victorian Britain* in *Photographica World*, number 69 (Bushey: The Photographic Collectors Club of Great Britain, June 1994).

Maurice, Phillipe, *Tintypes, snippets of history* in *PhotoResearcher* number 6 (Croydon: European Society for the history of photography, March 1997).

Mudd, James, *The collodio-albumen process, hints on composition and other papers* (London: Thomas Piper, 1866. OCR edition - LaVergne: Kessinger Publishing, 2008).
Richter, Stefan, *The art of the daguerreotype* (London: Viking, 1989).
Robinson, Henry Peach, *The studio and what to do in it* (London: Piper & Carter, 1885, 1891. OCR edition - LaVergne: Kessinger Publishing, 2010).
Thomas, D B, *The first negatives: an account of the discovery and early use of the negative-positive photographic process* (London, Her Majesty's Stationery Office, 1964).
Wilson, George Washington, *A practical guide to the collodion process in photography: describing the method of obtaining collodion negatives and of printing them* (London and Aberdeen: Wilson, 1855. OCR edition - LaVergne: Kessinger Publishing, 2008).
Wood, John & Foresta, Merry A, *The art of the autochrome: the birth of colour photography* (Iowa City: University of Iowa Press, 1993).

Early formats and presentation

Darrah, William Culp, *The world of stereographs* (Gettysburg: W C Darrah, 1977)
Darrah, William Culp, *Cartes de visite in nineteenth century photography* (Gettysburg: W C Darrah, 1981).
Hannavy, John, *Case histories: the presentation of the Victorian photographic portrait 1840-1875* (Woodbridge: Antique Collectors' Club, 2005).
Linkman, Audrey, *Nineteenth century card formats in Britain* (London: RPS PhotoHistorian supplement 92, March 1991).
Mathews, Oliver, *The album of carte de visite and cabinet portrait photographs 1854-1914* (London: Reedminster Publications, 1974).
Wichard, Robin & Carol, *Victorian cartes de visite* (Princes Risborough: Shire, 1999) [SoG shelf mark: TB/POR 17].

Interpreting old photographs

Pols, Robert, *Family photographs 1860-1945* (Kew: Public Record Office, 2002) [SoG shelf mark: TB/POR 14].
Pols, Robert, *Looking at old photographs* (Bury: Federation of Family History Societies, 1998) [SoG shelf mark: TB/POR 18].
Shrimpton, Jayne, *How to get the most from family pictures* (London: Society of Genealogists, 2011) [SoG shelf mark: TB/POR 28 & PR/PHO].

Dating old photographs

Linkman, Audrey, *The expert guide to dating Victorian photographs* (Manchester: Greater Manchester County Record Office, 2000) [SoG shelf mark: Shelf 9].
Pols, Robert, *Dating nineteenth century photographs* (Bury: Federation of Family History Societies, 2005) [SoG shelf mark: TB/POR 15].
Pols, Robert, *Dating twentieth century photographs* (Bury: Federation of Family History Societies, 2005) [SoG shelf mark: TB/POR 23].
Shrimpton, Jayne, *Family photographs and how to date them* (Newbury: Countryside Books, 2008) [SoG shelf mark: TB/POR 20].

Caring for old photographs

Linkman, Audrey, *Caring for your family photographs at home* (Manchester, Documentary Photographic Archive, 1991) [SoG shelf mark: Textbook tracts box].
Martin, Elizabeth, *Collecting and preserving old photographs* (London: Collins, 1998) [SoG shelf mark: TB/POR 12].

Photographic equipment and suppliers

Hercock, Robert & Jones, George, *Silver by the ton: the history of Ilford Limited 1897-1979* (London: McGraw-Hill, 1979) [SoG shelf mark: PR/PHO].
James, Peter, *The photographic manufacturers and retailers in Birmingham 1849-1914* (London: RPS *PhotoHistorian* supplement 112, 1996).
Thomas, D B, *Cameras, photographs and accessories* (London: Her Majesty's Stationery Office, 1966).
White, Robert, *Discovering old cameras 1839-1939* (Princes Risborough: Shire, 1995).
White, Robert, *Photographic accessories 1890-1970* (Princes Risborough: Shire, 2002).

Researching a business

Orbell, John, *A guide to tracing the history of a business* (Aldershot: Gower Publishing, 1987).
Probert, Eric D, *Company and business records for family historians* (Bury: Federation of Family History Societies, 1994).

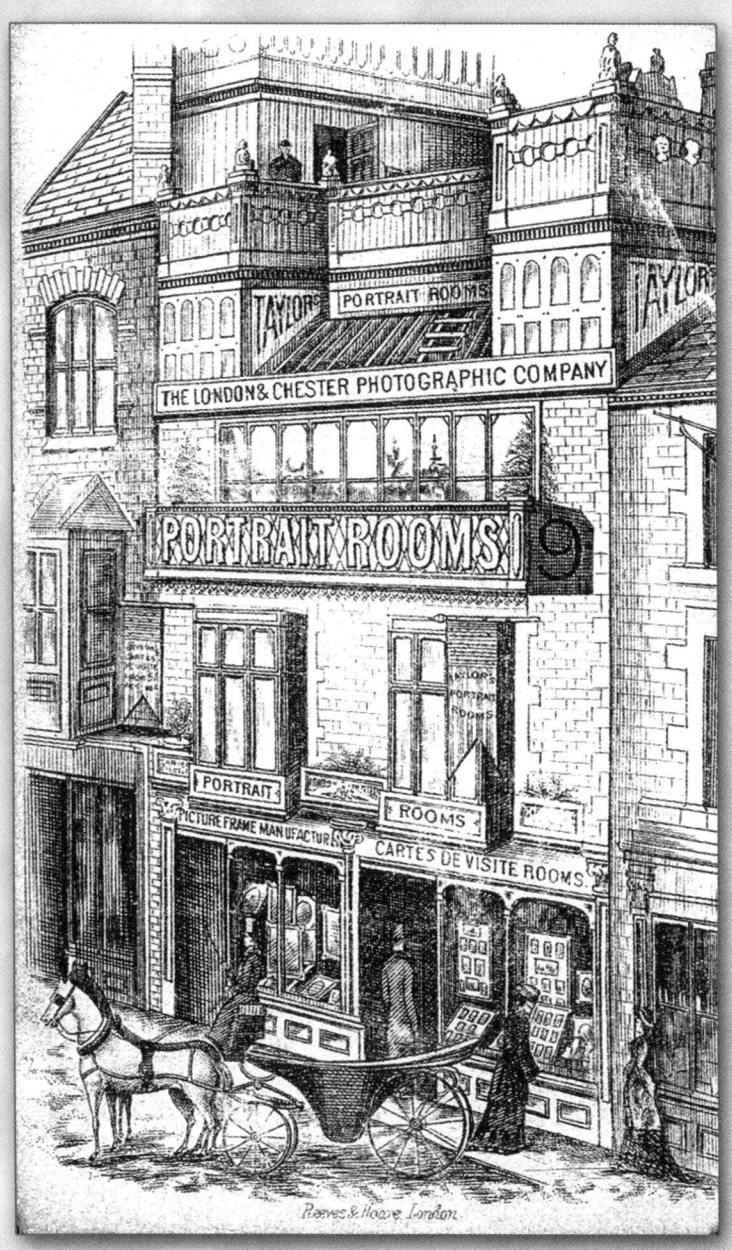

INDEX OF PHOTOGRAPHERS & PHOTOGRAPHIC SUPPLIERS

All photographers mentioned in the text, whether or not they were studio professionals, are included in this index, along with photographic innovators and suppliers. Occasionally, in one of the text's alphabetical lists, a photographer has been named for the sole purpose of providing a cross-reference to another more informative entry. In such instances, it is the page of the informative entry that appears in the index. Italicised page numbers refer to illustrations.

Abbey Studios	48	Bennett, Charles	6
Abery, P B	34, 58	Bennett, Mrs Charles	4
Alger, Cleer	37	Beresford, George	33
American Aristotype Company	7	Bevan, Henry William	39
Amey, William	112	Bird, Greystone	74
Annan, J Craig	58, 73	Bird, W S (*see* Sawyer & Bird)	
Annan, Thomas	33, 37, 73	Blair, John Price	74
Annan, T & R	67	Blanchard, Valentine	40, 67, 80
Archer, Frederick Scott	3, 145	Bliss, J E	40
Ashley, George & Abraham	37	Boak, Matthew	7
Ault, Frederick	74	Bolas, S B	39
Autotype Works	67	Bond, William	6
		Bone, May	8
Bagshaw, Luke	37, 58	Bool, Alfred & John	39
Baker, Harold	45	Booty, Abbott	55
Bale, Stewart	37	Boswell, William	80
Balmain, James C H	38	Bourne, Frederick	39
Banfield (*see* Foulsham & Banfield)		Bourne, Samuel	58, 74
Banyard, C	*131*, 132	Bowler, Chris	44
Barnes (*see* Brown, Barnes & Bell)		Bowness, J	132, *133*, 134
Barton, W Harvey	67	Bowness, Moses	74
Bassano, Alexander	33, 58, 67	Braddock, Alfred	39
Bassano & Vandyk	38	Brighton School of Photography	134, *136*
Baudoux, Ernest	38		
Baume, Messrs	55	Brookes, Warwick	58, *116*, 117
Beard, Richard	2, 58	Brookes, Warwick, Junior	117
Bedford, Francis	35, 67, 74, 80	Brookes, W & J	117
Begbie, Thomas	38, 58	Broom, Christina	59
Bell (*see* Brown, Barnes & Bell)		Brown, Barnes & Bell	6, 29, 67
Bell, Herbert	37	Brown, Theodore	59

Brunskill, J W	27	Ely, T H	2
Buckle, Samuel	54	Engelmann & Schneider	125
Buckley, Joseph	84	England, William	67
Burton, John	54	Everard, Blanquart	3
Bustin, Richard, Marion & William Henry	40	Farlie, Charles J	84
		Faulkner, Robert	67
Cameron, Julia Margaret	viii, 106	Fehrenbach, Emilian	84
Carbutt, John	7	Fergus, John	67
Carrick, William	59	Fisher, Walter	42
Cartland, G P	121, *122*	Fisher, William	14
Cartwright, R T	55	Flather, Henry	42
Chadwick, W I	74	Foot, Francis	33
Chaplin, Violet	51	Foulsham & Banfield	33
Chapman, J T	40, 74	Fowke, Charles Edward	42
Cherrill, Nelson King	30	Fox (*see* Maull & Fox)	
Clapperton, Robert	74, 107	Freeman, William Philip Barnes	42
Clarke, Bennett	74	Frith, Francis	34, 43, 52-3, 60, 75, 79
Clarke, John Palmer	40, 53, 59	Fry (*see* Elliott & Fry)	
Claudet, Antoine	2, 59, 74		
Coburn, Alvin Langdon	59, 74	Gibson, John Pattison	60
Coe, Albert Edward	74	Gill, William	71
Collie, William	38	Goddard, John	2
Collings, Arthur Albert	85	Goodrich, C E & Sanderson, F	40
Copsey, Ambrose	4	Graham, William	43
Corin, Walter	41	Greene, William Friese	54, 85
Cowell	41	Grove (*see* Window & Grove)	
Cundall, William	59	Gunn & Stuart	119
Daguerre, Louis	1, 2, 145	Hammond, Miss	123
Daines	54	Hardman, Edward Chambré	43
Davies, Peter	14	Hardman, Joseph	43
Delamotte, Phillip	75	Harries, D C	34, 75
Disderi, André	4	Harrison, William Marsden	75
Dixon, Henry	41	Harwood, William	34
Doran family	41	Hatch, Vincent	111
Doull, David	41	Hawkins, Mr & Mrs Charles	134, *136*, 137
Downey, William	75	Hayes, William	7, 60, 106-7
Downey, W & D	34, 67, 75	Henderson, Alexander L	75
Drummond, John	75	Hickox, Herbert Edward	44
Dubisson, Walter	4	Hills, Robert	55
Dunham, Percival	38	(*see also* Hills & Saunders)	
Dyche, Ernest	35	Hills & Saunders	53, 57
		Hinton, Alfred	88
Eason, Arthur	41	Hollyer, Frederick	33, 34, 44, 75
Eastman, George	7, 144	Hoppé, Emil Otto	60, 75, 80
Edis, Olive	33, 42, 59	Howard, Thomas	14
Edwards, B J	59	Howe, H L	60
Elliott & Fry	33, 60, 67, 125	Howlett, Robert	75, 83

Hughes, Jabez	67, 79	Mayall, John	4, 33, 67, 76
Hughes, Joseph	53, 60	Mayland, William	67
Humphreys & Whaite	113, *114*	Metcalf, Charles	39
		Midwinter, W H	67
Ilford Ltd	7, 155	Mitchell, William & William McLean	76
Jackson, Magnus	44, 61, 75	Moffatt, John	33, 61
James, A	*156*	Monte family	76
Jamieson, J H	137, *138*	Moss, William Dennis	46
Jarman, Harry	44	Mudd, James T	76
Jennings, Payne	67, 75	Mullins, Henry	38
Jubilee Photo Company	*156*	Münch (*see* Trapp & Münch)	
Jury, John	71	Muspratt, Helen (*see* Ramsey & Muspratt)	
		Muybridge, Eadweard	61, 85
Keene, Richard	61		
Kent, Tom	44	Newton, Sydney	76
Kevis, Walter	45	Nicholls, Arthur	40, 117
Knighton, Alfred	6, 14	Nicholls, Horace W	61
Knights-Whittome, David	45	Niépce, Nicéphore	145
Kodak	94, 144	Nunn, Cyril	62
Lafayette, James (*see* Lauder, James)		Orient Art Company	12
Lafayette Ltd (Manchester)	45	Ouless, Clarence	38
Lafosse, Augustus	67		
Lance, Frank	45	Parkes, Alexander	7
Lauder, James	33, 34, 76	Parrott, Edward	46
Laws, P Maitland	67	Payne, Edward Nixon & Jack Newsam	47
Lee, Nicholas	40	Pendle, Henry	4
Lemere, Harry Bedford	34, 45	Platinotype Company	67
Lewis, Arthur	34	Plowright, Walter Cole	47
Lewis, Thomas	61	Polyblank (*see* Maull, Henry)	
Light, Graham	46	Porter, Miss	123
Lock, Samuel	76	Prout, Victor Albert	76
Lofts, Peter	40		
London & Chester Photographic Company	*157*	Ramsey, Lettice & Muspratt, Helen	40, 53
		Read, Alfred	125
London Stereoscopic Company	76	Ream, Lilian	47, 53-4, 62, 76
Longstaff, Alice	41	Reason, Peter	46
Lösel, Franz Heinrich	76	Reeve, Lewis	123
Lumière Brothers	9	Reeves, Alfred	76
Lunn, Colin	40	Reeves, Edward	76
		Rejlander, Oscar	62, 77, 79
MacLean, Jane	6	Rey, Guido	44
Maddox, Richard Leach	5	Righton, John William	62
Mallinson, J	46	Roberts, Rousham	
Marion & Co	113, 121	(*see* Roberts, Thomas & Henry)	
Martin, Paul	vii, 61	Roberts, Thomas & Henry	48
Maull, Henry (including Maull & Fox and Maull & Polyblank)	33, 46	Robinson, Henry Peach	vii, 57, 62, 67, 79, *139*, 140, 141, 154

Rodger, Thomas	48
Roper, George	46
Russell, James	125
Russell & Sons	67
Salmon, Sidney C	48
Sanderson E (*see* Goodrich & Sanderson)	
Sarony, Oliver	vii, 2, 24, 62, 65
Savory, F Mortimer	48
Saunders, James	128, *130*, 132
Saunders, John Henry	
(*see* Hills & Saunders)	
Sawyer, J R	112
(*see also* Sawyer & Bird)	
Sawyer & Bird	5, 67
Schneider (*see* Engelmann & Schneider)	
Scorer, William	77
Scrivens, Leonard	62
Seaman, Alfred	52, 77, 79
Seavey, L W	125, 140
Shaw, John William & Alfred	48, 62
Short, J G & E G	113, *115*, 17, 119
Shrubsole, William	7
Silvy, Camille	33, 63, 127
Slingsby, Robert	67
Smith, Albert	38
Smith, Sarah & Percy	49
Smith, Thomas	8
Spalding, Fred & family	49, 63
Spanton, William & William Silas	44, 63
Speight, Edward Hall	63, 77
Speight, James x,	49, 123
Spinner, Frederick	38
Stabler, Paul	77
Stoneman, Walter	33
Stortz, Philip Christian	77
Stuart, William Slade	119
Stuart, W & J	119, *120*
Sturdee, Thankful	63
Sutcliffe, Frank Meadow	vii, 49, 57, 63-4, 77, 106
Sweetland family	84
Talbot, William Henry Fox	1, 2, 3, 101, 106, 152
Taunt, Henry	34, 64, 77
Taylor, A & G	6, 29, 67, 77
Taylor, Bert Armond	12
Thomas, John	34, 64, 77

Thomson, John	50, 64, 77
Tilley, H H	42
Titshall, Leonard & Ralph	64
Trapp & Münch	113, 119
Tunny, James Good	50, 64, 78, 94
Turner, Mr	123
Valentine, James	50, 64, 67
Van der Weyde	67
Vandyk, Carl	33
(*see also* Bassano & Vandyk)	
Vick, William	50
Walker, Samuel	*118*, 119
Walmsley, Charles	37
Wane, Marshall	67
Watkins, Herbert	33
Watson, Tom	50-1
Weiss, Paul	42
Welchman, Edgar & Son	51
Welsh, Robert John	78
Wenham, Francis	80
Went, Douglas	51
Whaite (*see* Humphreys & Whaite)	
Whitfield, George	78
Whitlock, Henry	65, 78
Whyte, David	51
Willey, Joseph	65
Williams, T R	78
Wilson, Christopher	39, 51, 65
Wilson, George Washington	33, 51-2, 65, 134, *135*, 154
Window & Grove	67
Wiseman, S	128, *129*, 132
Wood, William Hugh	52
Wood & Son	52
Woodbury, Walter	67, 80
Wright, Alfred & Hannah	78
Wright, Jasper James	x, 7, 8, 112, 123
Yerbury family	65
York & Son	78
Youens	54

GENERAL INDEX

Some explanation is necessary. Topics that already appear on the contents page as chapter or sub-chapter headings are not indexed, except where they are also mentioned on pages outside their eponymous habitat. Items that appear – and are easily findable – as part of a systematic list (such as individual studio directories or photographic societies) do not appear again here. Sometimes, however, systematic listing can hide topics: alphabetical lists based on author's name or website title do not necessarily reveal anything about content. A researcher seeking references to early photographers in Leeds, for example, would not automatically search under 'B' for 'Budge, Adrian'. In such cases, topics have been indexed in the normal way. Finally, a repository is listed only when there is some general comment on its holdings. It is not indexed if it is merely named as the home of an item that appears on a systematic list or is indexed in its own right.

Abe Books	ix
Aberdeen	134
Aberystwyth	71, 81
Access to Archives	55, 56
accessibility of records	31
advertisements	12, 14, 15, 89
affordability of photographs	2, 3, 4, 5, 8, 14
albumen paper	3, 5, 79, 124, 137, 154
albums	4, 9
Amateur Photographer	88, 90
Amateur Photographer and Photographic News	88, 90
Amazon	ix
Ambleside	132
ambrotype	3, 5, 144, 153
antique fairs	110
Archives Hub	55, 56, 79
Archon	55, 56
art and photography	
art photography	vii, viii, 69, 82, 88, 119, 140
status of photography as art	93, 112, 113
art nouveau	137
autochrome	9, 154
bankruptcy	90
Bath	19, 66, 134
Belfast Gazette	90
bibliographies	152
Birkenhead	89
Birmingham	66, 89, 101
Birmingham Central Library	35, 88
Birmingham Photographic Society	35
Blackpool	83
blogs	148-9
Bridlington	7, 147
Brighton	66, 82, 134
Bristol	55, 66
Bristol Record Office	54
British Association	101
British Humanities Index	89
British Institute of Professional Photographers	vii, 35

British Journal of Photography 88-9, 98
British Journal Photographic 88, 89
Almanac Photographer's Daily Companion
British Library 12, 16, 19, 32-3, 69, 90, 91, 106, 102
catalogue 87
Bromsgrove 53
Brown, John v
Brunel v
Burne-Jones, Edward 44
business associations 13
business records vi-vii, 111, 155

cabinet print 4, 5, 8, 9, 80, 109, 111, 117, 119, 154
calotype 2, 153
Camborne 80
Cambridge 40, 53, 66, 117
Cambridgeshire 2, 9, 40, 54
camera 91, 113, 124, 146
Box Brownie 7-8
box camera 7
carte de visite camera 146
carbon printing 3, 5, 94, 124, 137
Cardiff 89
care of photographs 148, 155
carte de visite 4, 5, 8, 9, 109, 111, 113, 119, 121, 128, 132, 134, 146, 154
cased images 145, 154
celluloid 7
census v, x, 12, 14, 18
Chelmsford 49
Cheltenham 66, 68, 113
Cheltenham Local Studies Centre 68
Chester 66
children 80, 112, 117, 119, 127, 134
chromotype 111
chrysotype 153
church events 13
cinema 85
Cirencester 46, 48
civic involvement 13, 112, 121
Clapperton Studio 107
collodio-chloride paper 7
collodion 3, 5, 6, 67, 125, 145, 154
colouring 14, 111, 119
commemorative pictures 127
Commonwealth photographers 84

composition 123, 128, 132, 134, 140
conventions 124, 126, 127, 128, 134, 137, 140, 141
copies 111, 117
copyright records 32
Cornucopia 55, 56
Creak's Almanack 15

daguerreotype 1, 2, 5, 71, 145, 153, 154
Daily Herald Archive 36
dating photographs v, 13, 17, 109, 125, 132, 134, 144, 148, 155
De Montfort University 102
death notices 12
Derbyshire 80
Devon 70, 80
digitised texts 147
Dimbola Lodge Museum 106
diorama 153
Diss 37
Dresden 125
dry plate process 5-6
Dublin Gazette 90
Dundee and East of Scotland 89
Photographic Association

East Anglia x
Eastbourne 39
Edinburgh 81
Edinburgh Gazette 90
Edinburgh Photographic 93-94, 103
Society
EdinPhoto 98, 103
Edwardian society 71
electricity 6-7, 13, 119, 124
Ely 14, 15
employees vii, 123, 125
enlargement 14, 111, 117, 119
Essex 66
Exeter 66, 71
exhibitions 90, 112, 121, 140, 148
exposure times 2, 80, 123, 126, 128

fading 124
Fakenham 8, 123
Falmouth 117
ferrotype (*see* tintype)
Fingerpost 15
finishing (*see* processing)

163

First World War	9, 137	Ipswich	41
fleamarkets	110	Ireland	89, 103, 144
focus	123, 124, 128, 132, 134, 140	Isle of Wight	71, 106
Fox Talbot Museum	106	itinerant photographers	vii, 2, 5, 12, 64, 153
formats	143, 144-5		
frame makers	80		
Frankwell	46	Jersey	38
Fylde, the	83	Jerwood Charitable Foundation	33
Fyvie	v	Johnson, Dr	106
gelatin-chloride paper	7	Kent Archives Service	54
Giant's Causeway	106	Kettering	6, 14
Glasgow	37, 43, 68	King's Lynn	2, 4, 7, 8, 15, 112, 123
Glasshouse Street	14	Kodak Museum	36
Glossop Dale Photographic Society	89		
Gloucestershire	80	Lacock Abbey	106
Gloucestershire Archives	68	Lakeland	70
Golden Jubilee	121	Lancashire	117
Google Books	88	Landport	112
Great Eastern	v	Leamington Spa	54
Great Exhibition (1851)	101	Leeds	66, 68
Great Yarmouth	2, 4, 12, 14, 15, 125	Leicester	66
group photographs	8, 127, 134	Leicester and Rutland Record Office	54
Guildhall Library	15, 19, 102		
		library services	ix, 15, 87, 89, 110
Harrogate	66	licences	2, 111
Harrow	53	Lincolnshire	66
Hayes Studio	106-7	Linked Ring	69, 140
Hereford	40	Liverpool	66
Hertfordshire	81	*Liverpool and Manchester Photographic Journal*	88
High Wycombe	84		
Historical Directories project	15	*Liverpool Photographic Journal*	88
History of Photography	88, 89	Local Government Act (1972)	17
history of photography	143-144, 145, 152	local history	16
		local publications	15
Huddersfield	111	London	vi, 2, 14, 15, 19, 39, 41, 50, 66, 83, 90, 101, 103
Hull	66		
Hunstanton	8, 123	London and Provincial Photographic Association	89
Hutton-le-Hole	7, 107		
		London Gazette	90, 103-4
Ilchester	68	Lowestoft	39, 51, 128
Imperial War Museum	34-5	Lyndhurst	113
International Exhibition (1862)	102		
International Museum of Photography	89	Manchester	66, 117
Internet Archives	88, 89	managing the subject	126-7, 128, 132, 134, 140
interpreting photographs	109-10, 148, 154		
		Margate	147
interviewing relatives	11	marketing	14, 111-113, 117, 119, 121
Inverness	51	niche markets	112, 119

Matlock (and Matlock Bath) 85
medals   101, 104, 112, 117, 119,
               121, 140
Metropolitan and District Railway   42
Midland Counties Photographic   35
   Federation

National Archives   16, 32
National Library of Wales   34
National Media Museum   36, 98, 105
National Monuments Record Centre   34
National Portrait Gallery   33, 80
National Register of Archives   55, 99
negatives   1, 2, 3, 7, 67, 94, 111,
               119, 123
new formats   8, 13
New Woman   137
New York   125
newspapers   12-13
Newsplan   12
Norfolk   x, 2, 4, 9, 132, 147
Norfolk Record Office   98
North of England Newspaper Archive   12
North Walsham   6
Northampton   4
Norwich   2, 6, 7, 4, 42,
               66, 112
Norwich Photographic Society   98
Nottingham   66, 70
Nottinghamshire   51

obituaries   12
opaltype   5, 8
optical character recognition   ix
orientalism   119
Orkney   52, 44
outdoor pictures   123
Oxford   66
Oxfordshire Records Office   55

Paisley   19
Paris   103
partnerships   17, 18, 90
patents   88, 90
patrons   14, 112, 117, 119
Periodicals Index Online   89
Perthshire   52
Petworth   45
Philadelphia   7

'photogenic drawings'   101
Photogram   90
Photograms of the Year   90, 102
photographer
   (*see also* studio photographer)
   amateur   viii, 2, 7-8, 9, 88, 89,
                     90, 91, 93-94, 99-100
   as publisher   viii, 5, 8-9, 14, 81
   specialist   viii, 67
photographic chains   6
Photographic Collector   90
Photographic Convention of   79
   the United Kingdom
Photographic Journal   88
photographic journals   79, 101
photographic market   2, 5, 6, 8, 9
   (*see also* marketing)
photographic mounts   4, 9, 11, 13, 17,
                     18, 109, 124,149
   design   112-113, 117
   suppliers   113
Photographic News   88, 90-1
photographic printing   67
Photographic Society of Great Britain   89
Photographic Society   98, 101, 102, 121
   (of London)
Photographic Society of Scotland   103
photographic studios   152-3
   backgrounds   123, 124, 125, 128,
                     132, 137, 140, 146
   day-to-day practice   89, 123
   earliest   2, 69
   equipment   91, 101, 126, 146, 155
   furnishings   123, 124, 125, 126, 128,
                     132, 134, 137, 140, 146
   lighting   6-7, 13, 14, 67, 119,
                     124, 132, 137, 140
   premises   13, 14, 16, 17-18, 146
   studio directories   13
photographic suppliers   113, 119, 121,
                     125, 146, 145
Photographica World   91
PhotoHistorian   19, 31, 91
   PhotoHistorian Supplements   19, 91
PhotoLondon   vi
PhotoResearcher   35, 91
picture books   vi, 16, 110
Plymouth   66
Polytechnic Institute   2

Portsmouth	112	social mobility societies	15
posing aids	126, 128, 132, 134, 137	non-photographic	13
(*see also* managing the subject)		photographic	88-9, 101, 102
postcard	8-9, 81, 137	Society of Arts	101
Pre-Raphaelites	14	Society of Genealogists	15-6, 110
Preston	137	Soham	4
prices	5, 8, 67, 80, 102, 111	South London Photographic Society	89
print-on-demand	ix	Southampton	66, 128
print sizes	5	special offers	8
prison studios	67	Stafford	42
prizes	101	Stationers' Hall	32
processes	14, 89, 102, 111, 144-5, 147, 153-4	stereo photography	viii, 5, 145, 154
		stereotypes (*see* conventions)	
processing and finishing	7, 9, 123, 124-5	Stockport Photographic Society	45
Professional Photographers' Association	35	*Studies in Photography*	91-2
		studio photographer	
		allied occupations	4, 14
Red Book	15	as scholar	112
remaindered books	110	as scientist	93, 112, 113
retouching	123	definition of	vii-viii
roll film	7	membership of societies	93-4, 99
Royal Commonwealth Society	84	variant descriptions	12, 13
Royal Cornwall Polytechnic Society	117	work rate	111
		working hours	6-7, 67
Royal Photographic Society	vii, 18, 19, 35-6, 91, 98, 102, 121, 140	working overseas	70, 84
		Sudbury	4
Historical Group	91	Suffolk	9, 132, 147
Royal Society	1	Suitall postcards	49
royalty	68, 117	Sunderland	66
Queen Victoria	v, 4, 68, 112, 117, 119, 121	Sussex	84
		Sutcliffe Gallery	106
Prince Albert	4, 121	Swaffham	2, 47, 112, 123
Princess of Wales	14		
Royal Warrant	68, 90, 112, 117, 119, 134	Tate Gallery	35
Rugby	49	Tenby	70
		Thetford	4
salted paper	3, 145	tintype	5, 145, 153
Scarborough	vii, 2, 66	Tonbridge	84
Science Museum	36	trade directories	4, 9, 13-15, 17-18
library	103	trade plate	113
Scotland	103		
Scottish Archive Network	55	Ulster	71
Scottish National Photography Collection	33-4	University of Glasgow Library	103
		University of Leicester	15
Scottish Photography Bulletin	91-2	USA	5, 81, 83, 140
seaside photographs	8		
Sheffield	66, 89	Victoria and Albert Museum	34
		Vienna	103, 119

visiting repositories	ix, 31
vital records	12
walking pictures	8, 147
Warwickshire County Record Office	54
Watt, James	117
weather conditions	80, 111-2
web links	148-9
wedding photographs	8
Wells-next-the-Sea	14
Welsh counties	17
West Glamorgan Archives Service	55
West Midlands	12
Whitby	49
Wimbledon	44
Windsor	121
Wisbech	2
Wolverhampton	85
women photographers	x, 69, 83, 149
Woodburytype	5
Worcester	66
world fairs	103
Worthing	125
Wrexham	137
York	66, 107
Yorkshire	66, 68, 106
Yorkshire College	89

About the SOCIETY OF GENEALOGISTS

Founded in 1911 the Society of Genealogists (SoG) is Britain's premier family history organisation. The Society maintains a splendid genealogical library and education centre in Clerkenwell.

The Society's collections are particularly valuable for research before the start of civil registration of births marriages and deaths in 1837 but there is plenty for the beginner too. Anyone starting their family history can use the online census indexes or look for entries in birth, death and marriage online indexes in the free open community access area.

The Library contains Britain's largest collection of parish register copies, indexes and transcripts and many nonconformist registers. Most cover the period from the sixteenth century to 1837. Along with registers, the library holds local histories, copies of churchyard gravestone inscriptions, poll books, trade directories, census indexes and a wealth of information about the parishes where our ancestors lived.

Unique indexes include Boyd's Marriage Index with more than 7 million names compiled from 4300 churches between 1538-1837 and the Bernau Index with references to 4.5 million names in Chancery and other court proceedings. Also available are indexes of wills and marriage licences, and of apprentices and masters (1710-1774). Over the years the Society has rescued and made available records discarded by government departments and institutions but of great interest to family historians. These include records from the Bank of England, Trinity House and information on Teachers and Civil Servants.

Boyd's and other unique databases are published on line on **www.findmypast.com** and on the Society's own website **www.sog.org.uk**. There is free access to these and many other genealogical sites within the Library's Internet suite.

The Society is the ideal place to discover if a family history has already been researched with its huge collection of unique manuscript notes, extensive collections of past research and printed and unpublished family histories. If you expect to be carrying out family history research in the British Isles then membership is very worthwhile although non-members can use the library for a small search fee.

www.sog.org.uk

The Society of Genealogists is an educational charity. It holds study days, lectures, tutorials and evening classes and speakers from the Society regularly speak to groups around the country. The SoG runs workshops demonstrating computer programs of use to family historians. A diary of events and booking forms are available from the Society on 020 7553 3290 or on the website **www.sog.org.uk** .

Members enjoy free access to the Library, certain borrowing rights, free copies of the quarterly *Genealogists Magazine* and various discounts of publications, courses, postal searches along with free access to data on the members' area of our website.

More details about the Society can be found on its extensive website at **www.sog.org.uk**

For a free Membership Pack contact the Society at:

14 Charterhouse Buildings,
Goswell Road,
London EC1M 7BA.
Telephone: 020 7553 3291
Fax: 020 7250 1800

The Society is always happy to help with enquiries and the following contacts may be of assistance.

Library & shop hours:

Monday	Closed
Tuesday	10am - 6pm
Wednesday	10am - 6pm
Thursday	10am - 8pm
Friday	Closed
Saturday	10am - 6pm
Sunday	Closed

Contacts:

Membership
Tel: 020 7553 3291
Email: membership@sog.org.uk

Lectures & courses
Tel: 020 7553 3290
Email: events@sog.org.uk

Family history advice line
Tel: 020 7490 8911
See website for availability

SOCIETY OF GENEALOGISTS
The National Library & Education Centre for Family History

Other SoG titles...

£8.99

£8.50

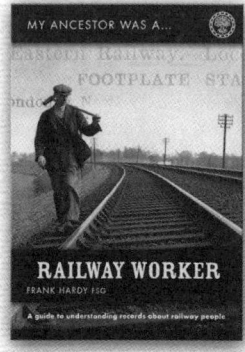
£7.50

£8.99

£9.50

£12.99

Order online at: www.sog.org.uk or call: 020 7702 5483.
Also available from the Society's bookshop.

14 Charterhouse Buildings, Goswell Road, London EC1M 7BA
Tel: 020 7251 8799 | Fax: 020 7250 1800 | www.sog.org.uk

Registered Charity No. 233701. Company limited by guarantee. Registered No. 115703.
Registered office, 14 Charterhouse Buildings, London, EC1M 7BA. Registered in England & Wales